JUST LOOK

95

5

JUST
LOOKING

Consumer culture in Dreiser, Gissing and Zola

Rachel Bowlby

Methuen
New York • London

First published in 1985 by
Methuen, Inc.
733 Third Avenue, New York
NY 10017

Published in Great Britain by
Methuen & Co. Ltd
11 New Fetter Lane,
London EC4P 4EE

© 1985 Rachel Bowlby

Printed in Great Britain
at the University Press,
Cambridge

Library of Congress Cataloging in Publication Data
Bowlby, Rachel, 1957–
   Just looking.
   Bibliography: p.
   Includes index.
   1. Fiction—19th century—History and criticism.
2. Fiction—20th century—History and criticism.
3. Naturalism in literature. 4. Consumption
(Economics) in literature. 5. Dreiser, Theodore,
1871–1945—Political and social views. 6. Gissing,
George, 1857–1903—Political and social views.
7. Zola, Emile, 1840–1902—Political and social
views.
I. Title.
PN3499.B64 1985 809.3'9355 84–27258
ISBN 0–416–37800–5
ISBN 0–416–37810–2 (pbk.)

British Library Cataloguing in Publication Data
Bowlby, Rachel
   Just looking: consumer culture in Dreiser,
Gissing and Zola.
   1. Fiction—19th century—History and criticism
   2. Fiction—20th century—History and criticism
   3. Consumers in literature
   I. Title
   809.3'9355   PN3499

ISBN 0–416–37800–5
ISBN 0–416–37810–2 Pbk

Contents

Illustrations

Illustrations

Acknowledgments

The research for this book was made possible by fellowships from the Georges Lurcy Foundation and Yale University. I would also like to express my gratitude to M. Simonnot of the Bon Marché department store in Paris and Pierre and Hélène Coustillas of the University of Lille for giving me open access to the archival materials at their disposal, and sharing their boundless enthusiasms for department stores and Gissing, respectively.

Hazel Carby, Michael Denning, Carla Freccero, Bob Horton, Raoul Ibarguen, Merrilyn Julian, Amy Kaplan, Rhoda McGraw, Reva Siegal and Gordon Turnbull were some of the friends who freely and warmly discussed, reacted and contributed. I owe much to my teachers at Yale, and am particularly conscious, and unconscious, of how much I have learned from Shoshana Felman and Fredric Jameson. Most of all, I thank Hillis Miller for his unstinting help, both scholarly and practical, at all stages.

A note on
texts and translations

For novels in English, I have used the most easily available edition in print. Extended passages from French novels and other texts have been translated, also some shorter quotations and phrases within the text where the sense of the passage might not otherwise be clear to a non-reader of French.

Epigraph

Mary Carmichael, I thought, still hovering at a little distance above the page, will have her work cut out for her merely as an observer. I am afraid indeed that she will be tempted to become, what I think the less interesting branch of the species – the naturalist-novelist, and not the contemplative . . . All these infintely obscure lives remain to be recorded, I said, addressing Mary Carmichael as if she were present; and went on in thought through the streets of London feeling in imagination the pressure of dumbness, the accumulation of unrecorded life, whether from the women at the street corners with their arms akimbo, and the rings embedded in their fat swollen fingers, talking with a gesticulation like the swing of Shakespeare's words; or from the violet-sellers and match-sellers and old crones stationed under doorways; or from drifting girls whose faces, like waves in sun and cloud, signal the coming of men and women and the flickering lights of shop windows. All that you will have to explore, I said to Mary Carmichael, holding your torch firm in your hand. Above all, you must illumine your own soul with its profundities and its shallows, and its vanities and its generosities, and say what your beauty means to you or your plainness, and what is your relation to the ever-changing and turning world of gloves and shoes and stuffs swaying up and down among the faint scents that come through chemists' bottles down arcades of dress material over a floor of pseudo-marble. For in imagination I had gone into a shop; it was laid with black and white paving; it was hung, astonishingly beautifully, with coloured ribbons. Mary Carmichael might well have a look at that in passing, I thought, for it is a sight that would lend itself to the pen as fittingly as any snowy peak or rocky gorge in the Andes. And there is the girl behind the counter too — I would as soon have her true history as the hundred and fiftieth life of Napoleon or seventieth study of Keats and his use of Miltonic inversion which old Professor Z and his like are now inditing.

Virginia Woolf.
A Room of One's Own

For Anna

1

Introduction

"L'Europe s'est déplacé pour voir des marchandises":[1] so commented the critic Hippolyte Taine in 1855, the year of the first Paris Exposition, and four years after the one at London's Crystal Palace which had started an international trend. The remark encapsulates the significance of the momentous changes in the scale and forms of commercial activity which had begun to take place at this time. No longer do goods come to the buyers, as they had done with itinerant hawkers, country markets or small local stores. Instead, it is the buyers who have taken themselves to the products: and not, in this case, to buy, but merely to "see" the things. In the late 1960s, Guy Debord wrote forcefully of the "spectacle de la marchandise." crystallizing the way that modern consumption is a matter not of basic items bought for definite needs, but of visual fascination and remarkable sights of things not found at home.[2] People go out of their way (*se déplacer*) to look at displays of the marvels of modern industrial production: there is nothing obviously functional in a tourist trip. And these exotic, non-essential goods are there to be seen by "tout le monde": no longer are luxuries a prerogative of the aristocracy. The great glass edifice of the Palace gives open access to all and marks the beginning of what would become, in one of the catch-phrases of the latter part of the century, "la démocratisation du luxe."

The grand buildings of the Universal Expositions, which took place in different cities of Europe and the United States every few years after Crystal Palace, bear a striking architectural resemblance to some more everyday "palaces of consumption." Department stores developed over the same period. Like the exhibition palaces, they utilized new inventions in glass technology, making possible large expanses of transparent display windows. Visibility inside was improved both by the increase in window area and by better forms of artificial lighting, culminating in electricity which was available from the 1880s. Glass and lighting also created a spectacular effect, a sense of theatrical excess coexisting with the simple availability of individual items for purchase. Commodities were put on show in an attractive guise, becoming unreal in that they were images set apart from everyday things, and real in that they were there to be bought and taken home to enhance the ordinary environment.

The second half of the nineteenth century witnessed a radical shift in the concerns of industry: from production to selling and from the satisfaction of stable needs to the invention of new desires. The process of commodification, whereby more and more goods, of more and more types, were offered for sale, marks the ascendancy of exchange value over use value, in Marx's terms. From now on, it is not so much the object in itself – what function it serves – which matters, as its novelty or attractiveness, how it stands out from other objects for sale. The commodity is a sign whose value is derived from its monetary price relative to other commodities, and not from any inherent properties of usefulness or necessity.

In France, the department store can be dated from virtually the same moment as the first Great Exhibition in London: the year 1852, when Aristide Boucicaut took over the Bon Marché. During the first eight years of his ownership turnover increased tenfold, and it went on rising at a comparable rate through the subsequent decades. The model was copied by other stores in Paris (Le Louvre, La Belle Jardinière, Le Printemps, Le Bazar de l'Hôtel de Ville, and others), in provincial cities and in other countries: Whiteley's and Harrods of London, Macy's of New York, Wanamaker's of Philadelphia, Marshall Field and The Fair in Chicago, and so on. Within a very short period, department stores had been established as one of the outstanding institutions in the economic and social life of the late nineteenth century; and together with advertising, which was also expanding rapidly, they marked the beginning of present-day consumer society. Stores, posters, brand-name goods, and ads in the daily and magazine press laid the groundwork of an economy in which selling and consumption, by the continual creation of new needs and new desires, became open to infinite expansion, along with the profits and productivity which lay behind them.

Some of the specific innovations which distinguished *le nouveau commerce*, as it was called, from the old have been outlined above. Grandiose architecture and theatrical forms of lighting and display contributed to a blurring of both functional and financial considerations, and other factors reinforced this effect. First, the inclusion of (potentially) every kind of object under the same roof removed the categorical distinction between different retailing specialities: the only characteristic unifying the goods in the store was that they were all for sale. Also, the client on her way from one department to another might well be attracted in passing by something which she had no previous intention of acquiring. "Impulse buying" replaced planned buying; or rather, as the chapter on Zola's *Au Bonheur des Dames* will show, the existence of such supposedly natural, irrational urges in customers was actually the result of a rigorously rational entrepreneurial scheme.

The principle of *entrée libre* or open entry did away with what had previously been a moral equation between entering a shop and making a purchase. At the same time, a fixed price policy, supported by clear labelling, put an end to the conventions of bargaining which focused attention on shopping as paying. Assistants in department stores received commissions on sales, so were inclined to be flattering rather than argumentative: the customer was now to be waited on rather than negotiated with and money, in appearance, was not part of the exchange (particularly since paying in fact took place in a separate part of the store). People could now come and go, to look and dream, perchance to buy, and shopping became a new bourgeois leisure activity – a way of pleasantly passing the time, like going to a play or visiting a museum. Stores became places where customers could even spend an entire day, since they were supplied with amenities ranging from reading rooms to refreshments to toilets – perhaps their nearest approach to basic use value. Thus the fantasy world of escape from dull domesticity was also, in another way, a second home. This combination would also tend to reinforce the potential for crossing the boundaries between looking and having: the real home could be made more of a fantasy place, the real woman more of a queen, just as the fantasy store was a place where she felt at home and enjoyed the democratic privilege of being treated like royalty.

All this is far enough from the steady serviceability of old-fashioned commerce. Perhaps most significant of all, the *prix unique* or fixed price also stood for cheapness, since rapid turnover of stock enabled the *grands magasins* to undercut their competitors with low profit margins. As Georges d'Avenel put it in 1894, "It seems that sales breed sales, and that the most diverse objects, juxtaposed in this way, lend each other mutual

---

Illustration 1 Interior of the Bon Marché, 1880. Like the grand railway stations built during the same period, department stores utilized the newly available steel and plate glass techniques to construct an image of openness, light and visibility. The palatial gallery with its chandeliers and tastefully arranged luxury merchandise produces a spectacle of aristocratic ease, where customers (and viewers of this drawing) are flattered by their own implicit inclusion.

support."[3] With the advent of the department store, selling takes on a life of its own, independent of the objects with which it deals, and by the same token, "shopping" as a distinctive pursuit has no inherent connection with the procuring of pre-determined requirements.

In the shift to consumer capitalism, then, modern commerce engages in a curiously double enterprise. On the one hand, a process of rationalization: the transformation of selling into an industry. The department stores are organized like factories, with hundreds of workers, shareholding companies, vast turn-overs, and careful calculation of continual strategies of expansion. On the other hand, the transformation of industry into a shop window. This massive and revolutionary extension of scope is achieved by the association of commerce with ideological values that seem to be diametrically opposed to the mundane actuality of work, profits and rationality. The *grands magasins*, like the great exhibitions, appear as places of culture, fantasy, *divertissement*, which the customer visits more for pleasure than necessity.[4]

The transformation of merchandise into a spectacle in fact suggests an analogy with an industry that developed fifty years after the first department stores: the cinema. In this case, the pleasure of looking, *just* looking, is itself the commodity for which money is paid. The image is all, and the spectator's interest, focused from the darkened auditorium onto the screen and its story, is not engaged by the productive organization which goes to construct the illusion before his/her eyes, nor with any practical use for the viewing experience. In the way it appears, the Hollywood "dream factory" necessarily suppresses

---

Illustration 2   Britain, 1880. According to the cautious principles of traditional commerce, the new businesses based on large-scale, low profit margins and expensive presentation techniques should have failed. The successful store owners in the cartoons play on the changed significance of these strategies, which can now be the means to success on an equally unprecedented scale.

THE DEPRESSION IN TRADE.

"I assure you, Miss, business is so bad that I have been compelled to enlarge my establishment and put larger plate-glass throughout."

"You'll believe me, Ma'am, at this price there is no profit whatever. I lose so much by it that I have been driven to the extremity of engaging two hundred extra assistants."

"My dear young lady, it was useless to struggle against fate. Business got *so* bad that I was positively forced to purchase this villa and *retire!*"

its mechanical, labored parts, and works against any notion of stable need by providing something characterized by its very separation from the relative ordinariness of everyday life.[5]

The dominance of signs and images, the elements of pleasure, entertainment and aesthetic appeal indicate what the new large-scale commerce shares with practices derived not from industrial production, but from the arts. Yet if industry, through the shift to selling techniques involving the making of beautiful images, was becoming more like art, so art at this time was taking on the rationalized structures of industry. In the period before cinema, the cultural industry *par excellence*, this is true most of all in the case of literary production.

The massive increase in book and journal output during the nineteenth century responded in part to a real change in market conditions: the increase in population and literacy. At the same time, reading became generally a private, domestic occupation, and one involving short-term rather than durable goods. These conditions implied a high volume and fast turnover of products, both of which were made possible by advances in technology and transport. More than at any time since the invention of printing and the beginnings of the first commodified literary genre, the novel, printed matter in general was becoming just another "novelty" to be devoured or consumed as fast as fashions changed. Production might in extreme cases be systematized to the extent of New York's "literary factories" which produced a regular quota of "written-by-the-yard" novels commissioned out to a list of competent workers.[6] In general, the rationalization of the publishing industry radically modified the status of writers, now greatly increased in number in proportion to the rise in output.

It is no coincidence that the "romantic genius" of the early part of the century came trailing his clouds of glory into the world at precisely the historical moment when the industrialization of literature could be read as a fatal compromise of his authorial freedom. Poetic genius pitted itself against the mechanical demands of an all-too-workaday commercial world, and neither side of the dichotomy, put this way, can be thought apart from the other. The same developments which were binding commerce and culture closer together, making commerce into a matter of beautiful images and culture into a matter of trade, a sector of commerce, also, paradoxically, led to the theoretical distinction whereby they were seen not just as heterogeneous terms but as antithetical in nature. The "absolute" value of "art for art's sake" versus the monetary values of commerce became a standard opposition in contemporary debates, and the difference between "authentic" and "enslaved" literary labor became a lived contradiction for working artists and writers throughout the century.

Naturalist novels stand at the crossroads of these concerns. Of the main genres of literature, itself the most industrialized of the arts, the novel was by far the most significant in terms of sales and the most systematically organized in its production and distribution. In the case of poetry, which was restricted to a limited readership of a certain class, and whose sales were rarely enough to pay the author a living wage, questions of the market were relatively insignificant. Poetry, as a result, could be identified as a place kept pure, the locus of "art for art's sake," uncontaminated by the profit motive or by the vulgar requirements of the popular market. In practice, only those with independent means of support could devote time to writing poetry; while scribblers of novels had their pages blotted both by the pressure to earn and to sell, and by the flimsy associations of something read predominantly by women with nothing different to do.

In refusing the theoretical opposition between art and the modern world, naturalists challenged the usual assumptions directly. Instead of the otherness of poetry, or the idealizing and moralistic tendencies of sentimental fiction, they took as their subject contemporary society, with all the qualities from the mundane to the brutal which allegedly made it incompatible with art. Technically, also, they adopted an explicitly modern method and language. Their work was researched as thoroughly as a sociologist's, and recorded for the most part in an objective, impersonal language. The period of naturalism (1880-1920, approximately) is contemporary with the rise of the social sciences, and there are significant parallels between the two practices. Their common project of showing the "facts" of society in a plain, unembellished form marked off naturalism as radically inartistic in the established sense, in which science and art were considered two poles as different from one another as machines from feelings.

In terms both of their place in the field of literary production, and of the methods and subjects which they took on, naturalist novels are thus on the borders between art and industry, which makes them *a priori* a promising ground for considering questions of commerce and culture in the late nineteenth century. These questions are also addressed directly and implicitly within the novels themselves, where they occur as part of the social reality which the novels seek to reproduce. Inside and outside the texts, then, these novels provide a way of exploring how such facts and values and changes are articulated into socially meaningful forms.

An issue which arises at every point is that of gender. Women's contradictory and crucial part in "the oldest trade in the world" – at once commodity, worker and (sometimes) entrepreneur – can be taken as emblematic of their significance in the modern commercial revolution. This is drawn out by a suggestive passage of Walter Benjamin's essay "Paris, capital of the nineteenth century" describing Baudelaire's dialectical images of "the ambiguity attending the social relationships and products of this epoch":

> Such an image are the arcades, which are both house and stars. Such an image is the prostitute, who is saleswoman and wares in one.[7]

From the point of view of the *flâneur*, the male stroller in the crowd, these are two analogous images of the ambiguity of modern consumption. For women, the contradictory experience has a further twist, involving a more than associative link between the two examples. It was above all to women that the new commerce made its appeal, urging and inviting them to procure its luxurious benefits and purchase sexually attractive images for themselves. They were to become in a sense like prostitutes in their active, commodified self-display, and also to take on the one role almost never theirs in actual prostitution: that of consumer. This gesture reinforced and extended existing tendencies whereby distinctions between "masculine" and "feminine" dispositions were constructed in terms of oppositions between work and leisure, rationality and emotion, practicality and the "instinct" for beauty.

These oppositions bear a striking resemblance to those engaged in the articulation of differences between commerce and culture, and in the latter field also, gender takes on a decisive significance. If culture, as a space marked off from business or working concerns, was also associated with femininity, that meant that being an artist might not sit well with a male identity. In the case of novels, as mentioned above, women were the main consumers, the main readers. The male novelist, then, might be in something of an ideological bind: neither pure artist nor fully masculine, and unable to alter one side of the pairing without damaging the other. Practicality in relation to the market meant catering to feeble feminine taste, while ignoring it meant withdrawing altogether from the normal conditions of masculine achievement.

In the section on commerce, Gissing's *Eve's Ransom* (1895) will be used as a basis to investigate key ideological paradigms connecting distinctions of gender with power and money and notions of culture as a locus of freedom. The forms of modern consumer subjectivity and the making of willing female consumers will be studied through Dreiser's *Sister Carrie* (1900) and Zola's *Au Bonheur des Dames* (1883). The section on culture will look first at modern literary production, via Gissing's *New Grub Street* (1891), then at the relation of art, business and sexual identity (Dreiser's *The "Genius"*, 1915), and finally at an argument for the novel as a possible middle way between the opposed values of art and the market (Zola's *L'Oeuvre*, 1886).

Taking texts by writers from three different countries at a comparable stage of social and economic development provides some indication of the range of positions and representations possible from within the common framework of early consumer society. The rationale behind the choice of these particular authors – rather than, for instance, Hardy, Howells and Huysmans – was simply to make the contrast of the three logically possible attitudes: broadly speaking, Dreiser, Gissing and Zola are (respectively) for, against and neutral with regard to contemporary developments in commerce and culture and their relations.

It is clear, however, that this kind of distinction cannot be taken in the abstract. Being American, with a different literary and intellectual tradition, inflects Dreiser's writing in certain ways, and the social conditions he describes are obviously not to be assimilated to those of Britain or France at the same time, despite underlying similarities. It could also be argued that there is nothing random about the connection of national origin and general attitude in each case. Certainly, enthusiasm for business innovations is more common among the American intelligentsia of this time than in England, where Gissing's brand of Arnoldian bitterness and irony has a peculiarly native look. Where appropriate, therefore, distinctions between the cultural histories of each country will be pointed out; the comparative framework is meant to indicate diversity as well as to show parallels.

But at the other extreme, differences between individual writers cannot simply be reduced to notions of national style, as if there were a homogeneous or median American, British or French ideology which each of them exemplified. Social class and ethnic, religious and educational background are also important (as are the differences in the meaning of each of these according to the society concerned), and no single factor can be treated as the key. Even if it might in theory be possible

12

to reconstitute and analyze the conditions that made Dreiser Dreiser – or, more precisely, made Dreiser's writings what they are – this would be justified only by an interest in Dreiser as a unique person or writer which does not apply for the purposes of this work.

Here, by contrast, the concern is with the novels as historically rather than biographically revealing. Read in conjunction with other forms of discursive evidence, they can be used to investigate how thinking around a pivotal question was organized; how that organization was related to the historical developments from which it derived and to which it gave, in turn, a sense, a meaningful form. It is in this sense that the novels are taken ideologically: as historically contingent and specific articulations of the world. This should make it clear that no static opposition of text to context or literature to background is invoked.

In an influential essay, "Narrate or describe?", on the difference between naturalism and its realist forerunners, Georg Lukács criticized naturalist novels for woodenly "sociological" tendencies to detailed description and specialized jargon. Unlike the earlier realist novels of Balzac, Dickens, Scott and Tolstoy, whose ideological engagement expressed "the inner poetry of life" and "the struggles of men in all their human complexity," the naturalist form reflects only the disillusionment of the bourgeois writer as passive observer of a reified world in which the sense of "vital relations" and "transformational possibilities" has been lost:

> The so-called action is only a thread on which the still lives are disposed in a superficial, ineffective, fortuitous sequence of isolated, static pictures . . . . The writer must strive to counteract the intrinsic monotony through the novelty of the objects depicted and the originality of the description.[8]

Yet the episodic structure of naturalist novels to which Lukács alludes with some deprecation here – "only a thread . . . a superficial . . . fortuitous sequence" – in fact suggests its

13

connection to the structures of experience in urban consumer society: to the positioning of subjects as viewers and consumers of "still lives" or "static pictures" seemingly without origin, to the seriality of fashion in the endless appearance of new images of "the new," and to the cycle of "monotony" and "novelty." The passage also suggests how novels themselves were like other commodities not only in their objective status as saleable goods, but in the "novel" experiences they promised.[9]

For Gissing and Zola, the role of external observer implied a necessary taking of distance in an attempt to acquire an objective and all-encompassing view or perspective. Personally, as in Gissing's case, authors might regret the impossibility of art providing a locus of stable or sacred value in the modern world of ephemeral, mass-produced art without "aura," to use Benjamin's terms, once "the technique of reproduction detached the reproduced object from the domain of tradition."[10]

But art could be forward- rather than backward-looking, and naturalism, accoding to Yves Chevrel, was nothing less than "a new way of conceptualizing the relations of literature to society" and one which "always shows an undeniable tendency to the breaking of boundaries."[11] Naturalism exposes society with all its flaws, all the seamy, distasteful corners into which a now by implication too genteel realism had failed to peer. The novels show or show up a multiplicity of social realities inconceivable as a single, unified whole. The slum, the suburb, the coal-mine, high finance, the theatre become the themes or fields of separate novels, each thoroughly noted and researched by the author as eye-witness – investigative reporter or sociologist – supplying "insider" information at once factual and sensational.

In 1765, Samuel Johnson had explained literary appeal in these terms:

> Nothing can please many and please long, but just representations of general nature . . . . The irregular combinations of fanciful

14

invention may delight a-while, by that novelty of which the common satiety of life sends us all in quest; but the pleasures of sudden wonder are soon exhausted, and the mind can only repose on the stability of truth. Shakespeare is above all writers . . . the poet that holds up to his readers a faithful mirror of manners and of life.[12]

For Johnson there remains a timeless truth against which to measure the superficial diversions of "novelty." At the end of the following century, novelty has taken over as the dominant mode or fashion against which the "repose" of a stable truth could only be an idealizing image or projection. For the naturalists there are relative truths, in the "local colour" and factual data of each milieu, any one or combination of which can be considered on its own terms. The mirror, no longer conceivable as "faithful" to an enduring or constant human nature, shows a fragmented image, or the image of one fragment in a world itself dominated by fluctuating, ephemeral images.[13]

As spectators of spectatorship, naturalist writers were not guilty of what Lukács calls a "passive capitulation" to their times. On the contrary, they saw that the representation of modern society must begin from the position of the viewer, that to gain a perspective on what *New Grub Street*'s Jasper Milvain calls "every department of modern life" was a matter less of "general nature" than specific areas, less of "just representations" than just, dispassionate looking. In this stronger sense, "just looking" imparts a second, surveying stage to the casualness of the random glance. Deliberately looking *into* a topic, or bringing to view a hitherto unrepresented portion of society, made naturalism seem less frivolous than the bulk of fictional literature being produced.[14] Plots that have only a semblance of narrative connection and completion often appear decidedly stilted or coincidental. But this reflects a necessity implicit in the irreconcilable doubleness of what Lukács identifies as the modern alternation of monotony and novelty, whereby events and changes cannot but seem random. The naturalists at once participate in and analyze the everyday subjective experience of being none other than an observer of a social reality that appears simply as a succession of separate images or scenes.[15]

The argument Lukács puts forward, objecting to the plethora of description and details at the expense of "proportions" and "order," is the radical side of a critical consensus which has habitually censured naturalist novels for their excessive confinement within their own period. It is ironic, in fact, that debates about literary naturalism, a form which assumed the priority of social determinations, have repeatedly focused on the question of whether particular authors deserve a place in the canon or whether their works are "merely" historical documents. Zola, for instance, has traditionally been relegated to a second rank in criticism of French literature: behind Balzac as a realist, and generally seen as too interested in the minutiae of factual exactitude to make him a truly literary creator. The fact that his novels have always sold well has not been a point in his favor, but has tended rather to reinforce the suspicious and somewhat immoral atmosphere surrounding the author of *Nana* and the like. Zola's literary rehabilitation over the past twenty years has often been effected through strategies which point out the complexity of mythological structures present in his works, or demonstrate how many passages in them use a language poetic enough to deserve close reading.[16] While this is necessary and stimulating work, it does not challenge the fundamental antinomy which opposes literary to historical, absolute to relative values. The information the novels supply about life during the Second Empire may be a useful source for historians, it is implied – and a valid one, given Zola's meticulous research – but literary interest will be established only by drawing out qualities of form, language, theme, structure and so on, which are taken as ahistorical.

Recently, new studies of naturalist writing have moved towards an articulation of literary and sociohistorical questions, and it is here that this book takes its context.[17] The valorization of "the literary" as such is itself a development of the nineteenth century, part of the general construction of culture in the artistic sense as a category in some way separate or exempt from social or economic determinations. And this polarization, as the second half of the book will try to show, is inseparable from the emergence of consumer culture.

2

Commerce
and femininity

Psychoanalysis was not the only enterprise around the turn of the century to be interested in the answer to Freud's famous question, "What does a woman want?" Women's desires and the objects of their investment were of the greatest interest and profit to the respected company Stuart Ewen dubs the "captains of consciousness."[1] His phrase is intended to evoke the transformation of business concerns from production to consumption – from concentration on the manufacture of goods under the management of the nineteenth-century captains of industry to the manufacture of minds disposed to buy them. The later captains of American industry, Ewen argues, were engaged in a deliberate endeavor to create the needs among potential buyers which would ensure the selling of the increasing quantities and types of commodity which their ever more efficient and productive factories were turning out. The use of distinctive brand names, display techniques and other means of advertising implied new methods of marketing aimed at selling the "image" of a product along with, or as part of, the thing itself.

The shift in the late nineteenth and early twentieth centuries to what is now conventionally known as "consumer society" was common to the countries of Dreiser, Gissing and Zola. Britain, France and the United States had the three highest per caput GNPs in the world at the beginning of this century; together with Germany, they were by far the most developed countries in terms of the scale of industrialization and their reliance on cheap raw materials imported from colonies. Despite individual variations in specific economic and cultural histories (American immigration, then at its height, clearly inflected developments in ways that did not apply to the European countries; France was far less affected by industrialization and urbanization in the nineteenth century than was Britain, and so on), it is reasonable to consider these states together, as occupiers of parallel positions in the world system, with cultural and ideological forms that can usefully be compared.[2]

As the proportion and volume of goods sold in stores rather than produced in the home increased, it was women, rather than men, who tended to have the job of purchasing them. Even though, particularly in the United States, large numbers of women were themselves beginning to enter the industrial wage-earning force, they also performed the services of housework and shopping for the home. More significant still, middle- and upper-class ladies were occupied with the beautification of both their homes and their own persons. The superfluous, frivolous associations of some of the new commodities, and the establishment of convenient stores that were both enticing and respectable, made shopping itself a new feminine leisure activity. On both counts – women's purchasing responsibilities and the availability of some of them for extra excursions into luxury – it follows that the organized effort of "producers" to sell to "consumers" would to a large measure take the form of a masculine appeal to women.

It does not matter in this regard how far individual capitalists or admen, or the fraternity as a whole, were conscious of this as a deliberate strategy (though Zola's *Au Bonheur* will present evidence to suggest that they certainly were in some cases); nor does it matter whether the modification of buying habits necessarily had the quality of intentional manipulation. The essential point is that the making of willing consumers readily fitted into the available ideological paradigm of a seduction of women by men, in which women would be addressed as yielding objects to the powerful male subject forming, and informing them of, their desires. The success of the capitalist sales project rested on the passive acceptance or complicity of its would-be buyers, and neither side of the developing relationship can be thought independently of the other.

On the other hand, women's consumption could be advocated unequivocally as a means towards the easing of their domestic lot and a token of growing emancipation. Elizabeth Cady Stanton punctuated her lectures of the 1850s with exemplary tales like the one about "The congressman's wife," an unfortunate soul possessed of an ill-equipped kitchen and a husband who complained about her cooking. Mrs Stanton's advice to her was:

> Go out and buy a new stove! Buy what you need! Buy while he's in Washington! When he returns and flies into a rage, you sit in a corner and weep. That will soften him! Then, when he tastes his food from the new stove, he will know you did the wise thing. When he sees you so much fresher, happier in your new kitchen, he will be delighted and the bills will be paid. I repeat – GO OUT AND BUY![3]

Illustration 3 The grand opening of Selfridge's in 1909 was preceded by a publicity campaign on a scale unprecedented in Britain. A former executive at Marshall Field in Chicago, Gordon Selfridge, used American marketing techniques to rival the profits and prestige of Harrods.

This image of the close and unequal bond between the "newest institution" and the woman presents it as a gift to her and a natural object for her protective regard. The store "dedicated to Woman's Service" seems to be answering to and subordinate to a pre-existing need or desire on the part of its female customers. Its future growth will indeed be in their hands.

SELFRIDGE'S London's New & Wonderful Shopping Centre ✠ ✠ ✠
Dedicated to Woman's Service - devoted to the Children's Needs - the Man's Best Buying Place - with best assorted Stocks at London's Lowest Prices:
NOW OPEN TO THE WORLD   OXFORD STREET LONDON.W.

F V POOLE 09

"London receiving her Newest Institution".

This apparently foolproof recipe – his fury, your tears, a nice meal, a "fresher, happier" you, then finally his conversion – is an interesting lesson in that much-vaunted nineteenth-century feminine power of "influence." Significantly, the injunction to buy comes from woman to woman, not from a man, and involves first bypassing and then mollifying a male authority. To "go out" and buy invokes a relative emancipation in women's active role as consumers. Given the assignment of women to the domestic sphere, shopping did take them out of the house to downtown areas formerly out of bounds, and labor-saving equipment could make home work more manageable.

At first sight there is a distinction between consumption for use and luxury consumption. A loaf of bread, in a society where bread is part of the staple diet, can hardly be considered an object of wishful desire on the part of its purchasers; a stove facilitates the performance of a socially necessary task. Women's relation to the materials of cooking and housework might, in fact, be the same as that of laborers or artisans to the tools required for their work.

Recent debates in Marxist and feminist theory, usually taking as their starting point Engels' *Origin of the Family, Private Property and the State* (1884), have addressed the issue of the ambivalent position of women in terms of social class and the relations of production. Engels argued that women's position in the modern family was analogous to that of the worker under capitalism, with the husband/father in the position of the capitalist exploiter of labor power. The theory referred to above, according to which housewives are equivalent to workers, stresses from another angle that homes perform the function of reproducing labor power: they are part of the infrastructure that maintains the male breadwinners as operative in their jobs.

But differences in the roles fulfilled by working-class and bourgeois wives – the unpaid domestic servant and the lady of leisure – immediately put in question the priority of gender to class in determining the social position of women. This can be identified either with that of the family wage-earner or with that of all women, considered as finally subject to patriarchal domination, whether their function be primarily industrious or ornamental. Women's ambivalent status is intensified by the consideration that large numbers of them became (low-paid) members of the workforce during this period. This made them on the one hand doubly exploited, contributing to capital's surplus at both labor and retail ends; and on the other, divided between the roles of masculine wage-earner and feminine housekeeper and consumer.

In a lucid exposition of the complexities of contemporary debates, Michèle Barrett concludes that it is neither possible nor useful to look for a simple formulation that would account for the place of "woman" as a generic or homogeneous social category.[5] Rather, the various analytical perspectives demanded by the different and often contradictory parts played by women in the society, and by the concept of "woman" in ideological constructions, must be used and examined in conjunction. There are risks involved in easy assimilations which can only mask the problematic and inconsistent nature of the various social and ideological positions woman/women may occupy in given social formations and in different historical periods.

No more straightforward is the status of those objects which women consume. A loaf of bread always provides a given quantity of nutrition, just as a vacuum cleaner presumably gets the cleaning done. But a selling process which involves competition between different brands of bread is necessarily engaged in presenting one particular type of loaf as superior to or different from its competitors. In the post-sliced-bread era, a loaf may be marketed as being uniquely nutritious; as containing some special ingredient; as the natural choice of the decent housewife ("Mother's Pride"); or as particularly good for slimmers (an interesting inversion of its original use, which can claim the reduction of calorific content, the amount of energy-producing food, as a positive quality). Clearly, if bread was not a source of food, no loaves would ever have been baked or sold. But the values attributed and added to it, whether in actual changes of substance or in the mental associations of the name or the image "sold" with the bread, raise it, with yeast of magical properties, to a status that exceeds (though it may still include) the functional. Need and kneading go together only up to a certain point.

In part, this development is instituted from the moment that any article of use ceases to be produced in the household and enters the market as a commodity with a price. At that point, as Marx describes in the opening chapter of *Capital*, its value must necessarily be estimated in relation to other, qualitatively different, objects, by means of the "universally equivalent form" which is money.[6] "The language of money" speaks the value of the commodity in terms which have nothing to do with its particular material aspects or relative utility.

Marx illustrates this point through the example of a coat and a piece of linen, two things which are obviously qualitatively different in terms of use, but come to acquire a definitely expressible relation when they are sold as commodities resulting from measurably different quantities of human labor time:

> When it is in value-relation with the linen, the coat counts qualitatively as the equal of the linen, it counts as a thing of the same nature, because it is a value . . . Yet the coat itself, the physical aspect of the coat-commodity, is purely a use-value. A coat as such no more expresses value than does the first piece of linen we come across. This proves only that within its value-relation to the linen, the coat signifies more than it does outside it, just as some men count for more inside a gold-braided uniform than they do otherwise.[7]

Cut off from its specificity or heterogeneity by entry into the commodity market, the object is free to be invested with properties real or imagined which may enhance its desirability, and hence its monetary standing, by comparison with other objects competing for the finite supply of purchasers' money.

Commerce and femininity

Following Roland Barthes Jean Baudrillard analyzes how this language of money and commodities has become an all-encompassing signifying system – the very texture of everyday forms of ideology.[8] In pre-capitalist society, there was an order of meaning in which things, gestures, work and activities were recognizably connected with a stable and functioning social ground. The ultimate effect of capitalism, Baudrillard claims, in its reified, consumer form, is to turn this system of use values into one of exchange values, characterized precisely by their arbitrariness in relation to the thing in question. All is (arbitrary) signs: we live in a structuralist universe where meanings are given by the relations of opposition and association existing between terms, and there is little possibility of getting beneath the surface layer of its system to see the supposedly existing reality – the real relations of people and things – beneath.

One of Baudrillard's illustrations of the distinction is the difference between *nature* and *naturalness*. For instance, a loaf of wholewheat bread is sold on the notion of naturalness. But this makes sense to the consumer not in some primary, self-evident way, but rather because the quality is presented as different from, an improvement on, the artificiality of a regular loaf – which only appears as artificial by its implicit definition as non-natural in relation to the wholewheat. It is thus impossible to speak, as does Daniel Boorstin in his dissection of the deceptive media forms of modern American consumer society, of a dichotomy between appearance, or *image*, and reality.[9] For this very distinction is in fact produced and deployed by the articulation of signs at a level removed from a reality that is necessarily inaccessible to it. Baudrillard puts the point in this way:

> One must guard against interpreting this massive enterprise for the production of artefact, "make-up," pseudo-objects, pseudo-events which invades our daily existence as a de-naturing or falsification of an authentic "content." It is in the form that everything has changed: everywhere there is substitution, instead and in place of the real, of a "neo-real" produced entirely out of the elements of the codes.[10]

There is a slight tendency in Baudrillard, with his opposition of "real" and "neo-real," to imply that pre-capitalist society is the authentic reality of grounded meaning, and thus to set up an alternative, historical dichotomy of "real" and "pseudo" which is not unlike those he unmasks in the synchronic codes of present-day society. But the structuralist model is a valuable one for examining the way that signs work in the codes of social signification. In showing as such, in its hidden limits, the framework within which individual choices and character traits are experienced as free, spontaneous and personal, the model of signifying systems makes possible the analysis of how meaning is produced, how codes can come to seem natural or true.

Baudrillard describes the way that the human subject in consumer capitalist society is objectified and fragmented, broken up according to the constantly changing demands of fashion. This consists of imperatives of consumption which ordain his or her mode of personal presentation in a thoroughly impersonal and objective manner:

> Everyone has to be up-to-date and recycle himself annually, monthly, seasonally in his clothes, his things, his car. If he doesn't, he is not a true citizen of consumer society.[11]

Like the car he owns, the individual is himself updated with regular new models, altering an identity assumed wholly through the things that his money can buy: clothes, cars and so on. The commodity makes the person and the person is, if not for sale, then an object whose value or status can be read off with accuracy in terms of the things he has and the behavioral codes he adopts.

The commodity can be anything at all, since it is defined not by any substance or given utility, but simply in virtue of the fact that it "goes to market," in Marx's phrase, with a price, a social value: it can as easily take the form of a person or a person's time as that of a physical object. To prove this point, Marx gives several playful examples in which commodity exchange involves the temporary or permanent sale of women:

Commodities cannot themselves go to market and perform exchanges in their own right. We must, therefore, have recourse to their guardians, who are the possessors of commodities. Commodities are things, and therefore lack the power to resist man. If they are unwilling, he can use force; in other words, he can take possession of them.*

* In the twelfth century, so renowned for its piety, very delicate things often appear among these commodities. Thus a French poet of the period enumerates among the commodities to be found in the fair of Lendit, alongside clothing, shoes, leather, implements of cultivation, skins, etc., also *femmes folles de leur corps*.**

** Wanton women.[12]

Not only can certain "wanton women" be sold, or sell themselves, as commodities, but the very imagery used of the relation between commodities and buyers is one of seduction and rape: commodities cannot ultimately "resist" the force of him who would "take possession of them."

This suggests that a productive channel of investigation might be opened up by considering what woman as ideological sign, and women as subjects caught or participating in various levels of social relations, have in common with commodities – with the things which a buyer consumes – and also, by looking at how women as consumers enter into reciprocal relationship with commodities. Marx's description of the consumer/commodity relation in sexual terms, as an appropriation of a passive object or body, may be juxtaposed with the empirical fact already noted that women, at the time when he wrote and increasingly over the next fifty years, were the principal consumers.

In dominant sexual codes, it is the woman's body which is taken by the man's; and more generally, it is the woman who is thought of as object or complement to the male subject. If she is herself the agent *vis-à-vis* the commodity, becoming, in this different context, a subject in a relation where she is elsewhere in the objective position, there is a seeming anomaly which provides one more indication of the conflicting places of woman and women in ideological and social practices. But Baudrillard's account of the consumer citizen suggests that the situation is even more complex. The consumer is not (just) an active appropriator of objects for sale. His or her entire identity, the constitution of the self as a social subject, a "citizen of consumer society," depends on the acquisition of appropriate objects: appropriate for the time (the seasons of fashion) and for the image which s/he is to project via the nuances of codes in dress and possessions – all the appurtenances of a "lifestyle" that can be recognized by other members of the society. There is thus a clear sense in which the consumer citizen is not so much possessor of as possessed by the commodities which one must have to be made or make oneself in the form objectively guaranteed as that of a social individual. What is by definition one's own, one's very identity or individuality, is at the same time something which has to be put on, acted or worn as an external appendage, *owned* as a property nominally apart from the bodily self.

In Marx's example, quoted above, about the soldier and his decorations, the man's identity is inseparable from the uniform which marks his status in relation to the (wearers of) other uniforms. The coat makes, is, the commodity; but where the relation of coat to linen draws both into the same qualitative category of comparable commodities with a money value, the uniform and the man fit together more tightly. The soldier without his clothes is beyond the pale, outside the semiotics of military status altogether. He would have another identity if differently dressed – for a different rank or as a civilian. But the naked man exposes himself to social ostracism. The sign is thus prerequisite to the personal identity it appears just to confirm rather than to confer. As with the commodity, there is no intrinsic value: the sign both produces and is the status given to the man, and it has a social sense on a level wholly separate from clothing.[13]

Baudrillard thus makes the argument that, in the same way that there is no nature in the codes of consumer society, but only the idea of naturalness, so there is no such thing as a person, but only the code or cult of "personality" or "personalization." This is constituted through the valorization of an authentic subjectivity actually acquired only through the objects which one owns and the habits one cultivates out of a limited set of options. Uniqueness has nothing to do with anything like an original character, just as in French the word *personne* is both "someone" and "no-one." The boundaries of subject and object, active and passive, owner and owned, unique and general, break down in this endless reflexive interplay of consumer and consumed. One consequence is that the clear separation of masculine and feminine roles as applied to the consumer/commodity relation cannot be maintained. It would seem, in fact, that in the priority of commodities to persons, the feminine commodity is in the dominant position – though the consequences of this for female consumers are evident.

The notion of "image" is useful for thinking about consumer forms of subjectivity. Significantly, it is a visual word harking back to the myth of Narcissus frustratedly gazing at himself in the pool. In Ovid's version of the story, recounted in the *Metamorphoses, imago* is the word used for the beloved reflection. In modern society, the image has other concrete and specific forms related to, but different from, the simple reflexive mirror relationship of self and self-image. Photography, cinema, billboard advertising were all being developed and coming to permeate social life in the period at the turn of the century. The photographic medium enabled a form of exact representation of places, people and things; in the multiple uses to which it was put, it both indicated and helped to promote a desire and willingness on the part of society to look at images of itself, collectively and individually – to see its own image reflected or refracted back through the technological medium.[14]

Narcissus' tragedy is that he cannot free himself from the

image with which he has fallen in love, which he wishes to grasp and possess and know (the Latin *comprendere* includes all three meanings), but cannot recognize as being only a derivative reflection of his own body. He is seduced by, and wants to seduce, something which is both the same as and different from himself, something both real and unreal: there to be seen but not tangible as a substantial, other body. It is an ideal image in which he sees nothing to threaten an unquestioning love. Narcissus is fatally caught inside a trap of attraction which he does not see to be of his own making, moving according to his own movements. The consumer is equally hooked on images which s/he takes for her own identity, but does not recognize as *not* of her own making.

Freud, writing during the early stages of the consumer period of capitalism, found in the Narcissus myth an apt evocation of one of the constitutive stages in the formation of human subjectivity, figuring the ego in its initial attachment to and identification with an ideal and all-fulfilling image both separate from and an extension of itself. The narcissistic stage is chronologically and structurally prior to the socialization of the child, who moves beyond the dyadic reflexivity of relation to the mother's body and his or her own potentially satisfying image, into the rules and practices of social convention. These are experienced as a limit to the child's omnipotence and self-sufficiency, but are ultimately internalized as the superego. In psychoanalytic terms, the impetus for this development is provided by the threat of castration. While boys can eventually respond to this by internalizing an active, moral identity modeled on their father's, girls must come to terms with the fact that they are already castrated, lacking the male organ and what it represents. If they do not, they are engaged in a futile attempt to take on the functions of a masculine subjectivity not their own. Hence the tendency of women to remain closer to the narcissism of childhood and outside the arenas of public achievement.

The point has often been made that Freud's account of

female subjectivity is overtly male-centred because of the significance attached to possessing the power associated with the phallus. His portrayal of women as defective males can be taken to demonstrate Freud's misogyny, considered either as a personal warp or, more generally, as a prejudice typical of his time and social class. Alternatively, the male bias of the work can be seen as a legitimate reflection of the hierarchy of sexual difference as it is in modern patriarchal society. As an interpretation of the implicit form of gender relations in Europe at the turn of the century, with more or less pertinence to other societies, Freud's description can then be allowed to stand.[15]

Such a perspective potentially offers a means of using Freud in a more historical way. Freud gives one kind of description of why it might be that women in bourgeois society are less active than men – less likely to leave the domestic sphere and, inversely, more narcissistically absorbed in themselves, their beauty, their desirability as potential objects of male love.[16] The determinants of this pattern are shown to exist within the nuclear family, which consists of a kind of cross-generational variant of the romantic love triangle – a structure which would itself, in Freud's theory, be a repetition in later life of the earlier family situation. Freud does not extensively address the relationship of the family to the social structure of which it is a part. If Freudian theory can be integrated into an understanding of the conditions of bourgeois society, there must be a relation between the passive, pre-social destiny of its anatomically female children, and wider forces governing the forms of familial and social experience in the society at large. The "family romance" is not the whole story.

Returning, then, to the question of the relation between women and commodities, there is an obvious connection between the figure of the narcissistic woman and the fact of women as consumers. "What does a woman want?" is a question to which the makers of marketable products from the earliest years of consumer society have sought to suggest an infinite variety of answers, appealing to her wish or need to

31

adorn herself as an object of beauty. The dominant ideology of feminine subjectivity in the late nineteenth century perfectly fitted woman to receive the advances of the seductive commodity offering to enhance her womanly attractions. Seducer and seduced, possessor and possessed of one another, women and commodities flaunt their images at one another in an amorous regard which both extends and reinforces the classical picture of the young girl gazing into the mirror in love with herself. The private, solipsistic fascination of the lady at home in her boudoir, or Narcissus at one with his image in the lake, moves out into the worldly, public allure of *publicité*, the outside solicitations of advertising.

"Just looking": the conventional apology for hesitation before a purchase in the shop expresses also the suspended moment of contemplation before the object for sale – the pause for *reflection* in which it is looked at in terms of how it would look on the looker. Consumer culture transforms the narcissistic mirror into a shop window, the *glass* which reflects an idealized image of the woman (or man) who stands before it, in the form of the model she could buy or become. Through the glass, the woman sees what she wants and what she wants to be.[17]

As both barrier and transparent substance, representing freedom of view joined to suspension of access, the shop window figures an ambivalent, powerful union of distance and

---

Illustration 4 Bon Marché appointments diary, 1889. The department store calendar redefines the months of the year according to featured categories of fashion. In the main body of the diary, these special events are noted along with holidays and religious festivals, integrating the new order of consumption into customers' lives. The diary acts as a daily reminder of the store's claim to attention, and also invokes a sense of personal involvement. Its owner identifies herself as a Bon Marché customer in a thoroughly individual way, inscribing her own plans on the printed pages.

AU BON MARCHÉ

Nouveautés
MAISON ARISTIDE BOUCICAUT

ATES DE NOS EXPOSITIONS & MISES EN VENTE
Dans le courant de l'année 1889.

Lundi 7 Janvier *et jours suivants*
MISE EN VENTE DES
COUPES DE ROBES
Coupons & Objets confectionnés
Largement diminués de prix.

LUNDI 4 FÉVRIER *et jours suivants*
Exposition et Grande Mise en Vente de
BLANC ET TOILES
CALICOT, LINGE DE TABLE, LINGE CONFECTIONNÉ
Trousseaux, Layettes, Lingerie fine
MOUCHOIRS, CHEMISES POUR HOMMES, BONNETERIE
Rideaux et Cretonnes pour Ameublements, etc.

Lundi 25 Février *et jours suivants*
EXPOSITION SPÉCIALE DE
GANTS et DENTELLES
FLEURS ET PLUMES
PARFUMERIE

Lundi 11, Mardi 12, Mercredi 13 Mars
Exposition générale et grande Mise en Vente
DES
NOUVEAUTÉS de la SAISON
Nombreuses Occasions à tous nos Comptoirs

Lundi 8 AVRIL *et jours suivants*
EXPOSITION SPÉCIALE DES
Costumes et Confections
VÊTEMENTS, CHAPEAUX ET CHAUSSURES
Pour Dames, Hommes et Enfants
Jupes, Jerseys, Peignoirs et Matinées, Ombrelles
OCCASIONS REMARQUABLES EN :
Soieries, Lainages, Fantaisie, Tissus imprimés pour Robes, etc.

LUNDI 6 MAI *et jours suivants*
EXPOSITION & GRANDE MISE EN VENTE
DES
TOILETTES D'ÉTÉ
pour Dames, Hommes et Enfants
Chapeaux et Ombrelles, Costumes de voyage
ÉTOFFES LÉGÈRES, TISSUS IMPRIMÉS
Articles de voyage, Ameublements pour la campagne.

LUNDI 3 JUIN *et jours suivants*
MISE EN VENTE DES
SOLDES ET OCCASIONS
en Nouveautés d'Été
Coupes de Robes, Coupons & Objets confectionnés
Largement diminués de Prix
Toilettes de campagne, Costumes de Bains de mer, Articles de voyage

---

Lundi 23 Septembre *et jours suivants*
EXPOSITION spéciale et Grande MISE en VENTE de
TAPIS
FRANÇAIS, ANGLAIS, D'ORIENT & DES INDES
Rideaux tout faits, Étoffes pour Ameublements
PORTIÈRES ET GALERIES ANCIENNES, SIÈGES DE FANTAISIE
Tapis de table, Broderies sur peluche
OBJETS DE LA CHINE ET DU JAPON.

Lundi 7, Mardi 8 et Mercredi 9 Octobre
Exposition Générale et grande Mise en Vente des
NOUVEAUTÉS D'HIVER
Affaires considérables et nombreuses Occasions
A TOUS NOS COMPTOIRS

Lundi 21 Octobre *et jours suivants*
Exposition spéciale des
TOILETTES D'HIVER
Manteaux, Robes, Jupes, Peignoirs, Fourrures
VÊTEMENTS, CHAPEAUX & CHAUSSURES
pour Dames, Hommes et Enfants
*Affaires exceptionnelles et nombreuses Occasions en
Soieries, Peluches, Velours, Lainages fantaisie et Lainages unis,
Draperie, Bonneterie, etc.*

Lundi 25 Novembre *et jours suivants*
MISE EN VENTE DES
SOLDES ET OCCASIONS
en Nouveautés d'Hiver
Coupes de robes, Coupons et Objets confectionnés
Largement diminués de prix
AFFAIRES EXCEPTIONNELLES
en Soieries, Lainages, Draperie, Fourrures
Bonneterie pour Dames, Hommes et Enfants, etc.

Lundi 2 Décembre
Ouverture de l'EXPOSITION des Objets pour
ÉTRENNES
ARTICLES de PARIS
Jouets
Maroquinerie, Petits Meubles, Objets de la Chine et du Japon
LIVRES D'ÉTRENNES

desire. Unlike Narcissus' reflection, the model in the window is something both real and other. It offers something more in the form of another, altered self, and one potentially obtainable via the payment of a stipulated price. But it also, by the same token, constitutes the looker as lacking, as being without "what it takes." Next year, or next door, at the superior establishment, the fashion will be different: the longing and lacking of the consumer are limitless, producing an insatiable interplay between deprivation and desire, between what the woman is (not) and what she might look like. The window smashes the illusion that there is a meaningful distinction in modern society between illusion and reality, fact and fantasy, fake and genuine images of self.[18]

3

Making up women: Gissing's *Eve's Ransom*

If Gissing himself was imbued with many idiosyncratic permutations of masculine identity, as his biographers have exhaustively described,[1] this does not prevent his writings from providing sharp analyses of the social forms and determinations of sexual difference in late Victorian Britain; and, conversely, of the integration of changing cultural practices and forms to existing systems of sexual difference. His short novel of 1895 brings together many of the contradictory representations of woman and women outlined in the introduction above. It shows how they were defined in conflicting ways by available ideologies but also capable, in that context, of developing strategies that might provide a relative independence from the norms of what a woman should be. The novel, as its title suggests, is concerned with women and money: with what money can buy, and with whether a woman is something for sale. It investigates the relation of Freud's question "What does a woman want?" to its other side, "What does a man want of a woman?" or "What does a man want a woman to want?" And it suggests that finally the answers to each, and the relevance of the questions, are themselves determined by wider social and ideological factors which offer particular and often incompatible forms of desire to men and women in what they expect of each other, and of themselves.

The plot of *Eve's Ransom* is set in motion by two events. Maurice Hilliard, the narrator, unexpectedly comes into a large sum of money in payment of a debt of honor by a formerly bankrupt business connection of his dead father. At the same time, he comes across a photograph of a woman named Eve Madeley, a relative of his landlady. The first circumstance represents to him the possibility of a radical alteration in his way of life, an "escape"[2] from his fairly menial position as a mechanical draughtsman. The second represents the image of "an ever-increasing suggestiveness of those qualities he desired in woman" (IV, 16). The money and the woman come together for Hilliard as means and end: means of release and object of pursuit; means of purchase and object to be bought. Each side of this odd doubling or coupling itself contains peculiarities.

Hilliard is not, even before his change of fortune, a stable, rooted character. Like so many of Gissing's heroes, he is a solitary, depressive semi-intellectual, situated in a kind of no-man's land between two social classes owing to an education "just sufficiently prolonged to unfit him for the tasks of an underling, yet not thorough enough to qualify him for professional life" (IV, 14).[3] He regards the job he does as his "servitude" (IV, 14), a "bondage to the gods of iron" (IV, 15); the four hundred pounds he receives will be enough to enable him "to live a man's life, for just as long as the money [will] last" (IX, 44). The sequel, as he subsequently explains to Eve, will be in one sense no different from the present, a simple return "back to slavery" (X, 45). But the interim will have functioned as a stabilizing influence:

> "I shall bear it more philosophically. It was making me a brute, but I think there'll be no more danger of that. The memory of civilization will abide with me. I shall remind myself that I was once a free man, and that will support me." (X, 45)

Hilliard sees things exclusively in terms of either/or oppositions: between freedom and slavery; between routine work and
leisure; between a life of choice and one of passive endurance
which can at best look for "support" from images of a "civilization" elsewhere and therefore, by definition, lost and unattain-
able in the here and now. The mechanical drudgery of
Hilliard's job is set against the aesthetic and hedonistic qualities
of other modes and places of existence: Paris, books, dining
out. The regular, repetitive earning of money (Hilliard receives
two pounds a week), eked out to support a female dependant as
well as himself, is contrasted to the quasi-magical status of the
debt money which comes in a lump sum, without connection to
the rational particulars of the means of its acquisition or expen-
diture.[4] In all these dichotomies, there is also a chronologically
grounded split. The ordered system of work and regularity,
quantitatively reducing the man to the hours he puts in and the
wages he gets for them, is the capitalist replacement of a pre-
industrial world which – from the nostalgic perspective of its
successor – appears as one of quality, value, "civilization":
authentic rather than enslaved experience.

It is this historical crossing, represented in Hilliard's concep-
tualization of his situation, which shows up in a different way in
the photograph of Eve Madeley he encounters in his landlady's
family album. It is on the one hand modern, the sign of a
technologically sophisticated era, its "likeness" mechanically
produced, with an exactitude of a kind not possible in a painting. It is also a sign of the democratization of art, beauty,
household possessions: the lower-middle-class Mrs Brewer
could not have paid for a portrait of her niece, nor, for other
reasons of class, would she have wanted one. On the other
hand, the photo, for all its realism, its portrayal of an actual,
individual human face, can conjure up associations and
idealizations of a type which would also have been projected
onto a vaguer, more stylized portrait of the traditional
kind.

Eve Madeley is a particular woman, but "Eve Madeley,"

whom Hilliard is told the picture represents, can acquire for him whatever characteristics he may happen, from his own disposition, to see in her image. The "half-sad, half-smiling face which so wrought upon his imagination" (IV, 19) transforms a Birmingham working girl into some enigmatic Mona Lisa or Petrarchan Laura. The literal uniqueness of Eve's features photographically reproduced (no two faces are the same) is accompanied by her picture's representation of a poetic or qualitative ideal of feminine "uniqueness": "to him it spoke as no other face had ever spoken" (IV, 17-18). Rational precision in the making of the object goes along with its capacity to inspire a non-rational imagining of an ideal type identified, like Hilliard's other oppositional categories, by its associations with a higher world apart from that of everyday existence.

The doubleness of the desires evoked in Hilliard by the combination of the money and the portrait of Eve leads to an indefinite pursuit in which he finally decides, "thinking and desiring and hoping he knew not what" (VI, 28), to track down the real Eve: not her photographic copy or the image it answers in his mind, but the living woman whose London address he has. The literal following of Eve in her outing to the Kensington Health Exhibition in fact comes after a different kind of pursuit, during the initial period of Hilliard's financial liberation, in which he is "possessed" by the dubiously euphemistic powers of "London's grossest lures" (V, 20). In contrast to city women, the provincial Eve Madeley now, in a sequence that makes sense in terms of Hilliard's abrupt alternations, becomes the explicit alternative to and diversion from the crudeness of what he had sought and what had entrapped him in the form of unadulterated sex appeal. Eve Madeley is made a maid, the anticipated embodiment of a feminine purity linked to the less corrupted world outside London from which, in Hilliard's social topography, she comes.

With such avowedly unreal expectations invested in her, Eve could at most chance to conform to Hilliard's hopes of "he knew not what." In practice, she is likely to fail what he sets up as an ultimate test in which, taking lodgings that look out on hers, he determines to "play the spy upon Eve's movements without scruple" (V, 25). In this relation, Eve is not so much an ideal to be contemplated as a potentially faulty object to be regarded with suspicion. But the ideal remains the criterion and there is a split between absolute perfection and objective signs of worldliness; between the enigmatic appearance or image, and the possibly dissolute physical woman automatically suspected of being involved in immoral behavior: "It was an odd thing that he constantly regarded Eve in the least favour-able light, giving weight to all the ill he conjectured in her" (XIV, 65). Hilliard follows the woman with the purpose of looking for incriminating evidence against the Eve who, in another way, he thinks of as flawless. Thus, after his first glimpse of her in the street, he speculates:

> She had the look, the tones, of one bent on enjoying herself, of one who habitually pursued pleasure, and that in its most urban forms . . . .
> Eve Madeley – the meek, the melancholy, the long-suffering, the pious – what did it all mean? (V, 25)

There is a further dimension to Hilliard's initial strategy. Spying places him in the supposedly impartial role of the unseen observer objectively viewing what goes on. But part of his confusion in seeing Eve arises out of the fact that she seems "altogether a more imposing young woman than he had pic-tured to himself" (V, 24) and evokes a physical response in him more akin, in his system of distinctions, to that of "London's grossest lures" than to that of the Dudley maiden:

> The interest she had hitherto excited in him was faint indeed compared with emotions such as this first glimpse of her had kindled and fanned. A sense of peril warned him to hold aloof; tumult of his senses rendered the warning useless. (V, 25)

The contradictory attitude of the spy or voyeur, at once aloof and bound to pursuit of the object, thus reflects a conflict or combination in Hilliard's mind between the driving power of lust and its "peril" which warns away. Eve, the woman, is both desirable and dangerous, to be seduced and a potential seducer herself.

But the division in Hilliard is actually, following the line of his compulsive gaze, projected outwards onto the figure of Eve, who is now looked upon as an almost intellectual puzzle to be solved: "the riddle of Eve's existence" (VII, 32); "a problem of which the interest would not easily be exhausted" (VII, 33). Starting from this perspective, it is only a short step to the stance which Hilliard adopts after he has finally introduced himself to Eve: that of her doctor, the one who will cure her problem.

The immediate cause of this is a request Eve makes for a loan of thirty-five pounds, her need of which is apparently linked to some dark secret involving an illicit relationship with a man. Hilliard agrees to give her the sum if she will give herself up entirely to him as a passive and powerless case to be healed:

> "I have come to the conclusion that you are suffering from an illness, the result of years of hardship and misery.... I am your physician; I undertake your cure. If you refuse to let me, there's an end of everything between us." (XII, 56-7)

Eve has thus shifted in Hilliard's representations from the status of an enigmatic image, "half-sad, half-smiling," to that of a "riddle" or "problem," at once abstract and objective, a thing to be analyzed and put right. The woman as enigma and the woman as temptress both affect the man, emotionally and physically; but as a physician, the man places himself in control of the woman, regarded as sick, inadequate, to be rectified and rendered acceptable and normal in his eyes. Structurally she is

---

Illustration 5   London shoppers and shop windows, 1908. Behind and in front of the glass, the spaces crowded with merchandise and people are virtually indistinguishable.

in the same position as that of the woman identified as a body, a thing to be sexually possessed; with the difference that the doctor goes one stage further in the process of objectification. He detaches himself from any subjective involvement, and identifies the capture or mastery of the object-woman with a change in its nature – or rather, a restoration from deviation – which is the "cure."

At the start of his paper on "Femininity" in the *New Introductory Lectures* of 1933, Freud raises the question of definition, using language strikingly similar to Gissing's:

> Throughout history people have knocked their heads against the riddle of the nature of femininity . . . . Nor will *you* have escaped worrying over this problem – those of you who are men; to those of you who are women this will not apply – you are yourselves the problem.[5]

In this period, it seems, the traditional "poetic" idealizations or mystifications of Woman as contradictory, mysterious, unknowable (Freud quotes some lines from Heine in the section omitted above) were being modified into a more scientific language of objectivity and objectification, in which women and their imagined essence of "femininity" became, as such, a medical "case" or problem.[6] As intellectual attitudes of the turn of the century, there is much in common between the analyst's enterprise and that of Gissing's hero, who sets out explicitly to "interpret Eve" (VI, 30).

The gesture of objectification is not a neutral one, and carries with it, in Gissing, more than a suggestion of sadism. To Eve's friend Patty Ringrose, who becomes the mediator and go-between for the physician and his designated patient, and expresses misgivings about Eve's physical capacity to comply with Hilliard's requirements ("But if she really *can't*"), he summarily replies: "Then it's her misfortune – she must suffer for it" (XIII, 61). And there is another component to their relation (one shared by the Freudian analyst, though in reverse) which is the money that Hilliard lays out, both in the payment of Eve's debt and in the carrying out of his prescription ("Your physician has ordered it," XIV, 66) of a forced vacation in Paris. The objective capacity of the money to purchase whatever may be considered necessary or desirable is inextricably linked to structures of gratitude, guilt and the sense of obligation, which dominate the relationship of Eve and Hilliard throughout the novel. "You feel the burden?" he eventually asks, when Eve voices her fear that she may be bound by "too much gratitude" (XIX, 90). And the sexual undercurrent of the exchange is brought out when the issue is temporarily resolved with a kiss signifying the monetary disparity between them:

> "Your gratitude be hanged! Pay me back with your lips – so – and so! Can't you understand that when my lips touch yours, I have a delight that would be well purchased with years of semi-starvation? What is it to me how I won you? You are mine for good and all – that's enough." (XIX, 90)

If, on one side, the curing of Eve engages a contract of love and money, paying for, and with, the woman's body, it also invokes an older myth of the chivalric rescue of a woman persecuted by an evil man: Eve's initial difficulties arise from her unwitting involvement with a married man, whose wife's debts she has been called upon to pay. In this case, it is not the literal saving of an innocent virgin, as with the knight on his charger and the damsel imprisoned in the castle, but rather a spiritual or moral saving of a woman who has lost her purity. Gissing's is a *fallen* Eve, an Eve who has succumbed to temptation. The fact that Gissing himself married a prostitute, and later a London working girl, with the hope that they could be "raised" to a decent life in his care, shows what a potent idea this was for him. By obeying Hilliard's orders and incurring a debt, Eve can be absolved from her sin, which is that of a whore; by paying him back with her lips, by becoming a whore, she can be absolved from her debt. Eve is caught in a bizarre tangle of female figurations which were all forceful in late Victorian

England but of very disparate ideological provenance: feudal debts of honor, Christian chastity and sin, romantic love, urban prostitution versus provincial innocence. She is the center of a problem which is not of her own making.

Gissing's novel deals exhaustively with the interlocking and contradictory projections to which the image of Eve is subject. The question of her identity, her "true" self, is continually posed by Hilliard; but since it is always in terms of his preconceived notions of what she was or ought to be like, there can be no definite answer: a comparative frame is in place from the start, with one Eve pitted against another, the photograph always held up as the reference for measuring her:

> "I want to hear you speak of yourself. As yet, I hardly know you, and I never shall unless you – "
>
> "Why should you know me?" she interrupted, in a voice of irritation.
>
> "Only because I wish it more than anything else. I have wished it from the day when I first saw your portrait."
>
> "Oh! That wretched portrait! I should be sorry if I thought it was at all like me."
>
> "It is both like and unlike," said Hilliard. "What I see of it in your face is the part of it that most pleases me."
>
> "And that isn't my real self at all."
>
> "Perhaps not. And yet, perhaps, you are mistaken. That is what I want to learn. From the portrait, I formed an idea of you. When I met you, it seemed to me that I was hopelessly astray; yet now I don't feel sure of it." (X, 48)

Hilliard is convinced that if he does not "know" Eve, Eve herself is not necessarily any more qualified to speak of her "real self"; and in taking on the function of her physician, he lays claim to a knowledge greater than hers of what is good for her.

Yet, as this passage reveals, there is also an Eve in the text who has her own notion of who she is: an Eve who in fact appears as "a woman who views life without embarrassment, without anxiety" (VI, 26). This impression, in the London railway compartment which gives Hilliard his first opportunity to "observe her at his leisure and compare her features with those represented in the photograph," is one of "strangeness" (VI, 26): it does not fit in with his view of the kind of bearing the subject of Mrs Brewer's photograph ought to show. But it is indicative of a self-possession and independence which other features of Eve's past life (as well as her face) express.

After her coping for a number of years as surrogate mother to her brothers and sisters in the absence of their alcoholic father, circumstances change and enable Eve to leave the Birmingham area for London, where she eventually finds a job as a book-keeping clerk on a pound a week. Like Hilliard, she has been given a chance of wider experience by an unexpected windfall – the finding of a cash-box, like the proverbial treasure chest, on Hampstead Heath, which she dutifully returns to the owner but for which she receives a reward of twenty pounds. Like Hilliard, her story as she tells it is one of personal liberation: "The change in me began when father came back to us, and I began to find my freedom. Then I wanted to get away, and to live by myself" (XVI, 75). She finds it impossible, however, to extricate herself from habits of thrift and self-denial, until her friend Patty "taught me to take life more easily. I was astonished to find how much enjoyment she could get out of an hour or two of liberty, with sixpence to spend" (XVI, 75).

As for Hilliard, the sudden influx of additional money takes on a psychological meaning; though in Eve's case only at the point when she has also lost her job:

> "All one night I lay awake, and when I got up in the morning I felt as if I was no longer my old self. I saw everything in a different way – felt altogether changed. I had made up my mind not to look for a new place, but to take my money out of the Post Office – I had more than twenty-five pounds there altogether – and spend it for my pleasure." (XVI, 76)

The differences from Hilliard's response are significant. In

Eve's case, earning a weekly wage itself represents an initial independence from confinement to the family home and the neighborhood where she was born, whereas Hilliard sees his job in terms of enslavement and thwarted ambitions. Eve combines regular work with judicious pleasures that vary with her means, as Patty's "sixpence" increases to opportunities for more visits to the shops, the theatre, the local library or even Paris (a place she had visited before she met Hilliard). Hilliard requires absolute freedom of action, a hedonistic abandonment of all that appears to him like the constraints of his usual social existence: "The only question is, how can I get most enjoyment?" (X, 46). His attitude to society, as to Eve, is one of superiority rather than acceptance. Books are not something he borrows from Mudie's to read and return, like Eve, but rather, as with the tome on French Gothic cathedrals he buys for five guineas, symbols of other and better things – the glories of old architecture and a bygone age – which he cherishes for that reason.

In the same way Aston Hall, where Hilliard has a rendezvous with Eve at one point, signifies for him the painful contrast between contemporary reality, as he sees it, and the past in which it was built:

From the eminence which late years have encompassed with a proletarian suburb, its once noble domain narrowed to the bare acres of a stinted breathing ground, Aston Hall looks forth upon joyless streets and fuming chimneys, a wide welter of squalid strife. Its walls, which bear the dints of roundhead cannonade, are blackened with ever-driving smoke; its crumbling gateway, opening aforetime upon a stately avenue of chestnuts, shakes as the steam-tram rushes by. Hilliard's imagination was both attracted and repelled by this relic of what he deemed a better age. He enjoyed the antique chambers, the winding staircases, the lordly gallery, with its dark old portraits and vast fireplaces, the dim-lighted nooks where one could hide alone and dream away the present; but in the end, reality threw scorn upon such pleasure. (XVIII, 82)

The contempt the narrator feels for reality is thrown back upon it in the reciprocal bitterness of reality's "scorn" projected by the solitary man who comforts himself with the power of the monument to let him "dream away the present." The ambivalent emotional attitude, "attracted and repelled," is at the same time a position of judgment, reproduced in the embittered irony of Hilliard's language when he takes Patty Ringrose on a tour of the Birmingham city center. The spectator separates himself in theory from a world which he both despises, wants to escape, and regards with fascination: "London's grossest lures" are gross but this is precisely what constitutes their appeal, their irresistible (al)lure.[7]

Hilliard's self-distancing position in relation to the sordid or blatantly industrial aspects of modern life – the "squalid strife," "fuming chimneys" and "proletarian suburb" – is, moreover, extended to what he sees of the upper-class world. Watching the carriages and red carpets of London's Woburn Square, he asks of Eve:

> "Does this kind of thing excite any ambition in you?" . . .
> "Yes, I suppose it does. At all events, it makes me feel discontented."
> "I have settled all that with myself. I am content to look on as if it were a play. These people have an idea of life quite different from mine. I shouldn't enjoy myself among them. You, perhaps, would." (X, 47-8)

The response to a show of "conspicuous consumption" – Thorstein Veblen's phrase for the affluent New York lifestyle of this period – is a denial of envy, a gesture of cool indifference which actually mimics the sophisticated detachment of those to whom it is directed. The dramatic reference also suggests the relaxation and passivity of a gentleman at the theatre. In both cases, the spectacles of working- and upper-class life, Hilliard's adopted stance of superior indifference or difference is imbued with a subjective element which he cannot escape, and which determines the form of his articulation of the escape or distance he claims. He hates and is drawn to the industrial world which makes him "a machine" and from which he comes; he suavely reduces to the unreality of a "play" the élite world from which the educated "underling" was excluded.

Hilliard preserves a solitary authenticity by the construction of oppositions, distancing himself from the world and distancing his world from its worthier historical antecedents. However, the terms of his abstract system have a definite relation to his own experience and place in that world. His ambivalently genuine/artificial position, or projection of it, is structurally similar to his various conflicting constructions of Eve. She is by turns image, reality, object or player of parts, in relation to himself as detached analyst, moral judge, interested physician, admirer, spy/spectator or enthralled pursuer. The complexity of Hilliard's formulations of his position as an individual in relation to society has much in common with his entangled engagement as a man with the Eve he takes to be "woman."

Eve, for her part, is not concerned with making rigid, hierarchical distinctions between different forms of life, between herself and society, or between herself and other people in it. She tends to accept things as they come, making use of what opportunities she has, as with her decision to go to London and her indulgence in modest pleasures. She does not look outside, or seek to stand apart from, the available boundaries and openings of a given stage of her life, but tells Hilliard that her chief interest is in "security":

> "Well, what do you aim at?" Hilliard asked disinterestedly.
> "Safety," was the prompt reply.
> "Safety? From what?"
> "From years of struggle to keep myself alive, and a miserable old age."
> "Then you might have said – a safety-match." (X, 46)

This unique glimmer of humor on Hilliard's part has an ironic fulfillment. Eve does not marry him but his old friend – and

48

only friend – Robert Narramore, an easy-going, effortlessly successful character who receives a legacy of five thousand pounds and deals in brass bedsteads. The security Eve seeks and achieves through marriage is unlike Hilliard's projected narrative of his life as a passage from slavery to freedom and back to slavery, after the money runs out. It contains no violent ruptures or alternations, and is rooted in gradually changing proportions and forms of work and leisure, carried on simultaneously and not represented in concepts of slavery versus freedom. Where Eve's "safety" means matching up and finding a stable place, Hilliard's aggressively oppositional system of thought is premised on the possibility/impossibility of breaking away, refusing to be assimilated to what he imagines not as a comfortable nest, but as a confining prison.

At another level, these differences can be represented in terms of active and passive tendencies, especially as they appear in the actual relations between Hilliard and Eve as man and woman. For Hilliard, Eve is something or someone to be known, mastered, possessed, bought, with money as the enabling medium, the necessary adjunct to his masculine power. Eve, in her "independence," working and living alone, looks upon money as a limited means to personal pleasures, and a form of insurance against possible future adversities: saving money is a contribution to safety. But her involvements with men deprive her of this self-sufficiency identified with the possession of money: the married man she meets transfers his debts to her, and this is what causes her dependence on Hilliard, her "burden" of "gratitude" after he pays them. She is caught in a double bind: the agreement is not a simple contract of loan and eventual repayment of a monetary sum, but requires that Eve, in return for his aid, do whatever Hilliard decrees as necessary to her "cure." The conditions thus entail that Eve give up liberty of action, become a slave of the ex-slave Hilliard and enter into his ideological universe consisting of relations of bondage and mastery. They also mean that she is doubly indebted financially (from the money he spends on her and Patty in Paris): her non-monetary repayment incurs yet more monetary indebtedness. Eve herself, in this exchange, becomes the monetary equivalent – in other words, a commodity. Hilliard acknowledges this negatively when he says, resigned to Narramore's victory: "One cannot purchase a woman's love" (XXII, 102). That, implicitly, is what he tried to do, and what Narramore, from one point of view, has done: his small fortune, pitted against Hilliard's dwindling four hundred and Eve's own twenty, clearly offers her more security. And it values her more highly.

In her position as both agent and commodity, Eve is indeed the site of an anomaly, or, in Hilliard's terms, a "problem." At the end, however, the contradictions seem to have disappeared. Eve's marriage gives her the "safety" she sought, "comfortably settled for life" (XXVII, 122). As "Mrs. Narramore, perfect in society's drill" (XXVII, 123), she has lost all vestiges of the uniqueness with which Hilliard originally invested her. The first time she and Hilliard meet after her marriage, the question of her identity is raised again, but now by Eve herself:

> "What am I, then?"
> "An English lady – with rather more intellect than most."
> Eve flushed with satisfaction. (XXVII, 123-4)

She is now, in both Hilliard's eyes and her own, a recognizable social average – a type. Eve has lost her individuality and become the mechanically reproduced aspect of the photograph, as is suggested by the detail which accompanies Narramore's informing Hilliard of the transfer of her loyalties: "The listener fixed his eye upon a copying-press, but without seeing it" (XXVI, 119).

If marrying Robert Narramore is the solution of "the riddle of Eve's existence," the end of the story leaves Hilliard wandering in country lanes, "a free man in his own conceit" (XXVII, 125). He too has risen a rung in social class, by entering an architect's office, and so remains, as in his initial liberation, "a machine no longer." Eve, meanwhile, has got herself covered with the desired "security" and become the contented, passive product of "society's drill," a happy machine. Given the problem, this is perhaps her only way out. Given a different problem, a different structure of relations and representations engaging men, money, power and women, the text, in its own dependence on "society's drill," would offer Eve a different apple.

4

Starring: Dreiser's
Sister Carrie

The curious rise of Carrie Meeber, provincial *ingénue* arriving on the train to find work in the Chicago of 1889 and ending as a star of the stage on Broadway, reverses the traditional tale of the fallen woman. Carrie's advance begins at the point where she succumbs to material need and goes to live with Drouet, the traveling salesman; her subsequent abduction by the sophisticated Hurstwood ultimately leads to her individual triumph in New York. She moves through successive stages: from subsistence-level worker in a shoe factory, to kept woman plus amateur actress; then kept woman cum housewife, as money decreases with Hurstwood; to professional actress supporting them both; until finally she is on her own as a highly paid celebrity.

Dreiser denies the significance of conventional morality in the making of human lives. Carrie is not helplessly tied to the fate of an old-fashioned virtue, the loss of which entails her own decline. Nor is she an active, assertive agent of her own success in the world, rationally assessing each situation or turning-point with an eye to the main chance. She makes it, but only to the extent that "it" makes her. She gets her lucky breaks, but with no more control than any woman fractured in a fortunate fall.

The version of social and subjective determination which Dreiser puts forward is encapsulated by a passage in chapter VIII which occurs at the point when Carrie has tacitly given in to Drouet by agreeing to go to lunch with him:

> Man is too intimate with the drag of unexplainable, invisible forces to doubt longer that the human mind is colored, moved, swept on by things which neither resound nor speak. . . . All that the individual imagines in contemplating a dazzling, alluring, or disturbing spectacle is created more by the spectacle than the mind observing it. These strange, insensible inflowings which alternate, reform, dissolve, are, we are beginning to see, foreshadowing the solution of Shakespeare's mystic line, "There are more things in heaven and earth, Horatio, than are dreamt of in your philosophy." We are, after all, more passive than active, more mirrors than engines, and the origin of human action has neither yet been measured nor calculated.[1]

Dreiser's reading of Herbert Spencer is evident here in the picture of the individual wholly subject to distant, "invisible forces" outside his or her control. What seems, however, the starkest, most anti-humanist environmental determinism is represented in the glowing poetic colors of "Shakespeare's mystic line" about Horatio, and "all that the individual imagines." In a world where everyone is a poet of "strange, insensible inflowings" there is none of Gissing's rage, but rather a celebration of the mysterious powers or materials that make minds into engines or mirrors, driven machines or passive reflectors.

Carrie's progress to stardom occurs in one sense between the two earthbound poles of the engine and the mirror, the operative in the factory and the actress adorning the pages of the Sunday newspaper. But there is a passivity involved in productive work for minimal wages, while the star as rich woman and as image for others seems to be more a source of active influence than the reverse. The two extremes interlock at every stage, up to and including that of Broadway, when Carrie is still, in some sense, a paid worker.

Even before she finds her first job, Carrie is given a view of

images beyond the mechanical engine. The seductive promises
of the city at the end of her train journey are later fulfilled in
the things she sees upon entering one of Chicago's new department stores, The Fair:[2]

> Carrie passed along the busy aisles, much affected by the
> remarkable displays of trinkets, dress goods, shoes, stationery,
> jewelry. Each separate counter was a show place of dazzling
> interest and attraction. She could not help feeling the claim of
> each trinket and valuable upon her personally and yet she did
> not stop. There was nothing there which she could not have
> used – nothing which she did not long to own. The dainty slip-
> pers and stockings, the delicately frilled skirts and petticoats,
> the laces, ribbons, hair-combs, purses, all touched her with
> individual desire, and she felt keenly the fact that not any of
> these things were in the range of her purchase. She was a work-
> seeker, an outcast without employment, one whom the average
> employé could tell at a glance was poor and in need of a
> situation. (III, 22)

Carrie is in a contradictory position, not only because she has
no money to buy things, but because she is in the store not to
look, but to look for work. She cannot, however, avoid the
influence, or "inflowings," of the articles which make their
"claim" upon her who cannot claim them. "Touched with
individual desire," Carrie's self is formed by concrete things in
a subjective image ("her personally") which she does not have
the means to make her own. She is an "outcast" not just
because she has no job, but because her identity is split between

---

Illustration 6 Pages from the 1895 catalogue of the Chicago mail
order firm Montgomery Ward, show the form in which tempting
displays of accessories and clothes, like those encountered by
Dreiser's Carrie, were transmitted to customers in regions distant
from the metropolis. With the illustration for visual appeal, the exact
quotation of prices, and the choice of more than one item in every
category, techniques of department store marketing are reproduced
in the book.

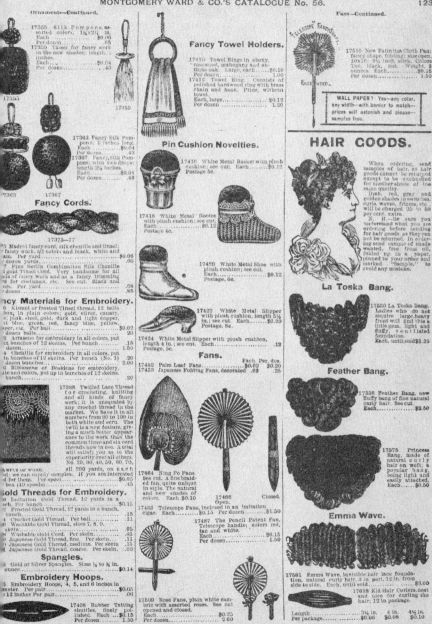

Ornaments—Continued.

17355   Silk Pompons, assorted colors, 1¼x2½ in.
Each.............................$0.06
Per dozen....................... .65
17359   Tassel for fancy work in the new shades; length, 3 inches.
Each.............................$0.04
Per dozen....................... .40

17363 Fancy Silk Pompons, 2 inches long.
Each.............................$0.04
Per dozen....................... .43
17367 Fancy Silk Pompons with two drops; length 2¼ inches.
Each.............................$0.04
Per dozen....................... .43

Fancy Cords.

17375—77
75 Madril fancy cord, silk chenille and tinsel; fancy work, all colors and black, white and ain. Per yard.................$0.06
 dozen yards........................ .60
7 Fine Berlin Combination Silk Chenille i gold Tinsel Cord. Very handsome for all ds of fancy work and as a fancy trimming it for costumes, etc. See cut. Black and ors. Per yard........................ .08
 dozen............................. .85

ncy Materials for Embroidery.

0 Kismet or frosted Tinsel thread, 12 balls box, in plain colors; gold, silver, canary, e, pink, steel, gold, dark and light copper, t blue, green, red, fancy blue, yellow, per, etc. Per ball..................$0.02
 dozen balls......................... .20
2 Arrasene for embroidery in all colors, put in bunches of 12 skeins. Per bunch...... .15
 dozen bunches...................... 1.50
4 Chenille for embroidery in all colors, put in bunches of 12 skeins. Per bunch (No. 1) .20
 dozen bunches...................... 2.00
6 Ribbosene or Braidene for embroidery, te in colors, put up in bunches of 12 skeins. bunch............................. .20

17388 Twilled Lace Thread for crocheting, knitting and all kinds of fancy work; it is unequaled by any crochet thread in the market. We have it in all numbers from 20 to 100 in both white and ecru. The twill is a new feature, giving a much better appearance to the work than the common three and six cord threads now in use. A trial will satisfy you as to the superiority over all others. No. 20, 30, 40, 50, 60, 70, all 200 yards, on each MPLE OF WORK. spool. If you are interested we can supply samples.
 d for them. Per spool..............$0.05
 box (10 spools).................... .45

old Threads for Embroidery.

0 Imitation Gold Thread, 12 yards in a ich. Per bunch.....................$0.15
2 Frosted Gold Thread, 12 yards in a bunch. bunch.............................. .15
4 Crochet Gold Thread. Per ball....... .13
6 Washable Gold Thread, sizes 7, 8, 9.
 skein.............................. .05
8 Washable Gold Cord. Per skein...... .05
1 Japanese Gold Thread, fine. Per skein. .11
0 Japanese Gold Thread, medium. Per skein .15
1 Japanese Gold Thread, coarse. Per skein. .20

Spangles.

3 Gold or Silver Spangles. Sizes ¼ to ⅜ in. ounce.............................$0.14

Embroidery Hoops.

3 Embroidery Hoops, 4, 5, and 6 inches in meter. Per pair.....................$0.05
 12 inches Per pair.................. .06

17408 Rubber Tatting shuttles, finely polished. Each $0.15
Per dozen.......................... 1.50

Fancy Towel Holders.

17410 Towel Rings in ebony, rosewood, mahogany and antique oak. Large, each.....$0.10
Per dozen.......................... 1.00
17412 Towel Ring. Consists of polished hardwood ring with brass chain and hook. Price, without towel.
Each, large,.....................$0.12
Per dozen 1.20

Pin Cushion Novelties.

17416 White Metal Basket with plush cushion; see cut. Each......$0.12
Postage 5c.

17418 White Metal Bootee with plush cushion; see cut.
Each.............................$0.12
Postage 4c.

17420 White Metal Shoe with plush cushion; see cut.
Each.............................$0.12
Postage, 6c.

17422 White Metal Slipper with plush cushion, length 5½ in.; see cut. Each.......$0.20
Postage, 8c.

17424 White Metal Slipper with plush cushion, length 4 in.; see cut..................... .12
Postage, 5c.

Fans.

Each. Per. doz.
17452 Palm Leaf Fans...........$0.02 $0.20
17453 Japanese Folding Fans, decorated .03   .25

17464 Ring Po Fans. See cut. A fine braided fan, quite unique in style. The natural and new shades of colors. Each.$0.10

17466   17466
Open.   Closed.

17466 Telescope Fans, inclosed in an imitation cigar. Each.....$0.15 Per dozen......$1.50
17487 The Pencil Patent Fan, Telescope handle; colors red, tan and white.
Each.............................$0.15
Per dozen.......................... 1.50

17509 Rose Fans, plain white cambric with assorted roses. See cut opened and closed.
Each.............................$0.25
Per dozen.......................... 2.60

17510 New Fatinitza Cloth Fan; fancy shape, folding; size open, 10x10; 9½ inch stick. Colors: Tan, black, red. Weight, 8 ounces. Each..............$0.15
Per dozen.......................... 1.50

WALL PAPER? Yes—any color, any width—with border to match—prices will astonish and please—samples free.

HAIR GOODS.

When ordering, send samples of hair, as hair goods cannot be returned except to be exchanged for another shade of the same quality.

Drab, red, gray and golden shades in switches, curls, waves, frizzes, etc., will be charged 25 to 50 per cent. extra.

N. B.—Be sure you understand what you are ordering before sending for hair goods as they cannot be returned. In ordering send sample of shade wanted, free from oil, folded up in a paper, pinned to your order and marked "Sample," to avoid any mistake.

La Toska Bang.

17530 La Toska Bang. Ladies who do not require large, heavy front will find this a little gem, light and fluffy. Ventilated foundation.
Each, until sold$1.25

Feather Bang.

17536 Feather Bang, new fluffy bang of fine natural curly hair. See cut.
Each..............................$2.50

17575   Princess Bang, made of natural curly hair on weft; a popular bang, being light and easily attached.
Each..............$0.50

Emma Wave.

17581 Emma Wave, invisible hair lace foundation, natural curly hair, 3 in. part, 12 in. front side to side. Each, until sold..........$3.00

17618 Kid Hair Curlers, neat and nice for curling the hair; 12 in package.

Length..............	3½ in.	4 in.	4½ in.
Per package........	$0.06	$0.08	$0.10

Bleached Cotton Flannel.

Per yard.
4520 Bleached Cotton Flannel, width 25
inches................................$0.06½
Price for full piece of about 58 yards, 9½ cents
per yard.
4522 Bleached Cotton Flannel, width 26 inches,
per yard.................................08½
Price for full piece of about 58 yards, 8¼ cents
per yard.
4524 Bleached Cotton Flannel, width 26 inches .10
Price for full piece of about 57 yards, 9½ cents
per yard.
4526 Bleached Cotton Flannel, width 28
inches.................................12
Price for full piece of about 55 yards, 11¼
cents per yard.
4528 Bleached Cotton Flannel, heavy weight,
width 28½ inches........................14
Price for full piece of about 55 yards, 13¼
cents per yard.

Cotton Flannel—Continued.

4530 Bleached Cotton Flannel, width 29½
inches, extra heavy.....................$0.15½
Price for full piece of about 54 yards, 15 cents
per yard.

Colored Cotton Flannel or Drapery Plushes.

Used for Portieres, Wall Hangings, Linings, etc.

Per yard
4550 Colored Cotton Flannel, old gold, medium
and navy blue, olive, wine, cardinal, scarlet,
drab or brown, 25½ inches...............$0.09
Price for full piece of about 54 yards, 8½ cents
per yard.
4554 Colored Cotton Flannels, high colors, blue,
scarlet, garnet, brown, slate, pink, drab and
gold, 27 inches.........................12½
Price for full piece of about 55 yards, 11½
cents per yard.

Drapery Plushes—Continued.

4556 Heavy Cotton Plushes, 28 inches wide:
plain colors: Cardinal, scarlet, wine, pink,
claret, blue, drab, slate, brown, old gold ... $0.1
Price for full piece of about 55 yards, 13 cents
per yard.

Fancy Colored Cotton Plush.

4560 Colored Cotton Flannel, black striped or
checked with scarlet, old gold checked with
black, width 27 inches..................$0.1
Price for full piece of about 56 yards, 9½ cents
per yard.

Use the William Clark Co.'s "N-E-W" Six Cord Spool Cotton.

LADIES' AND CHILDREN'S SUIT DEPARTMENT.

*Ready Made Wrappers and Tea Gowns; dresses made
to order.* Styles absolutely correct and up to date.
Note—We cannot furnish samples of wrappers or
other ready-made garments. Samples of any garments
which we quote to measure and make up in our custom department will be cheerfully sent upon request.
Special—We can make to order any dress shown in
the *Standard Fashion Catalogue.* Samples of dress
materials and any information desired will be fur-
nished upon request.
Write for our Special Dressmaking Catalogue No. E,
mailed free of charge.
See our Special Catalogue E for rules for measurement.
Ready made wrappers, gowns and dresses are made
in the following scale of sizes only:
Bust, 32 in. Length, 54 in. Bust, 38 in. Length, 58 in.
Bust, 34 in. Length, 56 in. Bust, 40 in. Length, 58 in.
Bust, 36 in. Length, 56 in. Bust, 42 in. Length, 58 in.

5610 Ladies' Ready
Made Wrappers, made
of high grade novelty
chintz, black grounds
with small neat floral
designs in colors, lined
waist, belt, Watteau
back, large sleeves
and wide cape ruffle
over shoulders, trim-
med with handsome
2-inch cream lace, the
prettiest garment ever
made for the price.
Each............$1.25
Per doz.......14.25

5614 Ladies' Wrapper, made
of Domett outing flannel in
narrow stripes: medium colors, lined waist, belt, full
back, large sleeves and wide
ruffle over shoulders, forming yoke.
Each....................$1.40
Per dozen.............16.25

5600 Ladies' Ready Made Wrappers, made of dark prints; new
styles; lined waist, belt, full
sleeves, wide ruffle over shoulders and forming pointed yoke.
Each....................$0.59
Per doz................6.65

5602 Ladies' Ready Made
Wrappers, made of indigo
blue prints, small and medium
figures, lined waist, large
sleeves, belt, wide ruffle over
shoulders and forming yoke.
Each....................$0.69
Per doz................7.85
5604 Ladies' Ready Made
Wrappers, made of fast black
prints, medium and small
white figures and stripes, lined
waist, belt, large sleeves,
wide ruffle over shoulders and
forming yoke, Watteau back.
Each....................$0.85
Per doz................9.75

5614-16

5616 Ladies' Ready Made
Wrapper, made of plain
fast black Henriett
sateen, lined waist, belt,
Watteau back, large sleeves,
wide ruffle over shoulders
forming yoke. Same style
as above.
Each....................$1.4
Per dozen............16.8
5618 Ladies' Wrapper,
made of cashmere de lain
in dark grounds with floral stripes in bright contrast-
ing colors, entirely new
has lined waist, belt,
Watteau back, leg of mut-
ton sleeves, circular ruffle.
Each....................$1.5
Per dozen............17.4

5618-20-22-24

5620 Ladies' Ready Made Wrappers, made of
new dark striped ginghams; same style as above.
Each....................................1.5
5622 Ladies' Ready Made Wrappers, made of
printed flannelette; handsome figured stripes
in dark colors. New goods. Same style as
above. Each...........................1.5
5624 Ladies' Ready Made Wrappers made of
cashmere flannelette; fleeced back, dark
grounds printed in bright mixed floral and Persian designs. Style same as above. Each....1.8

5611 Ladies' Ready Made
Wrappers, made of best
quality American indigo
prints, blue grounds with
neat white figures, yoke,
collar and cuffs of plain
indigo blue cloth trimmed
with narrow fancy
braid in blue and white,
has lined waist, belt, full
front and Watteau back and
shoulder ruffles.
Each......................$1.25
Per dozen....... 14.25

5611

5606 Ladies' Ready
Made Wrappers,
made of best Ameri-
can indigo blue
prints, same style as
above.
Each............$0.85
Per doz......9.75
5608 Ladies' Ready
Made Wrappers,
made of best qual-
can indigo blue or
fast black and white
prints, lined waist,
large sleeves, belt,
wide cape ruffle over
shoulders, Watteau
back, ruffle and col-
lar trimmed in nar-
row feather stitch-
ing.
Each............$0.98
Per doz......11.25

5608

5612 Ladies' Wrap-
pers, made of high
grade novelty chintz;
black grounds with
small figures or dots in
white or colors, such
as gold, blue, etc.,
lined waist, belt, Wat-
teau back, large sleeves,
ruffle over shoul-
ders forms pointed
yoke, ruffle trimmed
with two rows white
rickrack braid.
Each....................$1.10
Per dozen.......12.80

5612

5626 Ladies' Ready Made
Wrappers, made of dark figured sateen; black grounds
with small bright printed designs, lined waist, belt, Watteau back: new cape front
trimmed with cream lace in-
serting, large sleeves.
Each....................$1.75

5626

Ladies' Wrappers—Continued.

5627 Ladies' Ready Made Wrappers, made of medium and dark colored Persian striped flannelette, cashmere twilled surface with fine soft fleece on inside; lined waist; wide ruffle over shoulder, tapering to waist line in front and back; large drop sleeves and belt. Each................$1.50

5628 Ladies' Ready Made Wrappers, made of English cashmere, full wool. Colors: Navy blue, cardinal, wine or black; lined waist, full Watteau back, loose front led to form with small extra, large drop sleeves, embroidered collar and two rows embroidery scroll design worked in the material the entire length of front.
Each................$3.50

5629 Ladies' Ready Made Wrappers, made of half worsted brocaded suiting, ruffle of the same material over yoke front and back, large sleeve with ruffle at elbow, Watteau pleat from yoke; lined waist. Colors: Navy blue, tan, cardinal, light gray, brown, wine, myrtle or black. Each......$2.75

5630 Ladies' Ready Made House Wrappers, made of striped English flannelette, medium colors, pointed yoke and full back, held to the front with belt of the same material, revere front, raised shoulders, full ruffled sleeves. Each........$2.25

5632-34 Ladies' Ready Made House Wrappers, made of fast black flannelette sateen, full back and front shirred at collar, lined waist, raised shoulders. Each...........2.35

5634 Ladies' Ready Made Wrappers, same style as above, but made of small figured or striped black and white sateen. Each............2.50

Ladies' Tea Gowns.
Made to measure.

5650 Ladies' Tea Gowns, made of best English cashmere; black, cardinal, wine, navy or sapphire blue, full front and back, lined throughout, large colored sleeves, wide revere front, worsted braid trimming on collar, revere and sleeves. Each................$3.00

5652 Ladies' Tea Gowns, made of best English cashmere, black, wine, cardinal, navy or sapphire blue, light blue or pink, lined throughout, tight fitting waist in back with Watteau pleat from yoke, loose fitting, 22 or 24 button sleeves, epaulet shoulders and ruffle across front and back. Each................5.00

5654 Ladies' Tea Gown, made of all wool reversible crepe line twill, lined throughout, has large puff sleeves, wide ruffle and collar trimmed with narrow silk ribbon, full Watteau pleats in back from collar. Colors: Cardinal, wine, navy blue or black, or any other seasonable colors. Each................$6.50

5656 Ladies' Tea Gown, made of new illuminated twill suiting, lined throughout, has large sleeves, close fitted back and loose front lined to figure with half belt, velvet butterfly front and collar trimmed with lined braid. Colors: Wine, cardinal, navy, myrtle, brown or tan. Each................$6.75

5558 Ladies' Tea Gown, made of fine French Henrietta, lined throughout, handsome shirred front and back, ruffled collar and cuffs, sleeves with ruffle, shirred in arm hole, full Watteau full front trimmed with silk ribbon to match. We can furnish in navy, cardinal, wine, or any other seasonable shades. Each................$9.00

Children's and Misses' Dresses.

5680 Little Girls' Dresses, made of best staple gingham, small checks in navy blue, brown or pink, with white yoke of white all over locking, trimming of white Hamburg edging. Ages 2½ yrs., 3 yrs., 4 yrs., 5 yrs.
Each................$0.69

5682 Little Girl's Dress, made of small checked lady flannel, in pink, light blue, tan, scarlet or gray. The daintiest fabric you ever saw. Round yoke, wide circular ruffle, full bishop sleeve.

Ages	2½ yrs.	3 yrs.	4 yrs.	5 yrs.	6 yrs.
Price	$0.75	$0.88	$1.00	$1.10	$1.20	$1.30

5684 Little Girl's Dress, made of striped henrietta, in scarlet and black only. Small neat design in beads on scarlet grounds; full front with girdle, wide sash at back, full bishop sleeves, girdle, cuffs, collar and bottom of skirt trimmed in all wool black hercules braid.

Ages	2½ yrs.	4 yrs.	5 yrs.	6 yrs.	7 yrs.	8 yrs.	9 yrs.
Price	$1.25	$1.35	$1.45	$1.55	$1.75	$1.95	$2.15	$2.35

Ages 10 years, $2.50.

5686 Little Girl's Dress, made of English cashmere, half wool, wide pointed ruffle over shoulders to waist line forming V front and back, lined throughout, full bishop sleeves, cuffs, collar and ruffle trimmed in fancy silk braid, made in all seasonable colors.

Ages	3 yrs.	4 yrs.	6 yrs.	8 yrs.	10 yrs.	12 yrs.
Price	$2.75	$3.10	$3.45	$3.80	$4.15	$4.50

5688 Little Girl's Dress, made to measure as above, but of fine finished, all wool flannel, full bishop sleeve, lined waist only.

Ages	3 yrs.	4 yrs.	6 yrs.	8 yrs.	10 yrs.	12 yrs.
Price	$1.90	$2.20	$2.50	$3.00	$3.50	$3.95

5692 Misses' Dress, made of English cashmere, half wool, lined throughout, has round yoke formed by wide military cape ruffle extending across shoulder, full balloon sleeves, empire belt, collar, cuffs, ruffle, and bottom of skirt trimmed with worsted hercules braid. We can furnish all seasonable colors.

Ages	12 yrs.	13 yrs.	14 yrs.	15 yrs.	16 yrs.
	$5.00	$5.25	$5.50	$5.75	$6.00

5694 Misses' Dress, same style as above, made of fine all wool serge. All the staple and new shades.

Ages	12 yrs.	13 yrs.	14 yrs.	15 yrs.	16 yrs.
	$6.00	$6.25	$6.50	$6.75	$7.00

5696 Misses' Dress, made of one novelty suiting, wool bourette effects, combinations or dark colors intermixed. Waist is made over fitted lining. Three box seams are formed of the material in the back and front below a shirred yoke of velvet in shade to harmonize with goods, epaulets over shoulders ripple over the large mutton sleeve, narrow skirt, gored skirt. Color effects are in brown, green, wine or gray.

Price	12 yrs.	13 yrs.	14 yrs.	15 yrs.	16 yrs.
	$5.50	$5.75	$6.00	$6.25	$6.50

Ladies' Newport Suits.

See note under department heading for scale of sizes.

5700 Ladies' Newport Suit, ready made, consists of jacket and skirt to be worn with shirt waists. Jacket is made with Tuxedo back, turned or mutton sleeve, wide revers in front, double stitched seams, inside seams bound, gored skirt, very full and wide, deep turned hem at bottom. Made of good looking and serviceable repellent cloth, in navy blue or black. Per suit................$4.00

5702 Ladies' Newport Suit, same style as above. Made of sicilian repellent cloth. Collar, cuffs and bottom of skirt trimmed with black worsted hercules braid. Colors, black or navy blue only. Per suit................$5.50

5704 Ladies' Newport Suit, same style as above, made of heavy all wool storm serge, trimmed with two rows of folded satin duchesse on collar, cuffs and bottom of skirt. Colors: Black or navy blue only. A stylish and splendid wearing suit. Per suit................$5.95

Consequence of consumer goods on C.

resignation to self-denying subservience and a limitless desire for more things ("she did not stop"). The first involves a machine-like subsistence, the second a mirror-like self-display, resembling the one on the counters, that will alter the condescending looks of those who "could tell at a glance" she is not one of them. Carrie "felt keenly the fact" of her own falling (apart) between the dazzling shows of possibilities and the immediate, compelling need to find work in order simply to survive.

No option but to buy.

Carrie's exclusion from the world of the department store makes the opposition between necessity and "the drag of desire" (III, 23) stand out in stark relief. Precisely because she cannot pay for anything at all, she is cut off from the question of making a rational, considered choice between various options. It is the very inadequacy she feels because "not any of these things were in the range of her purchase" which allows her to wish without measure or calculation: "There was nothing there which she could not have used – nothing which she did not long to own."[3]

The combination of looking at a display of the things that money can buy and feeling excluded and inferior is repeated much later, when Carrie takes her first walk down Broadway in the company of her New York neighbor, Mrs Vance:

She was in fashion's throng, on parade in a showplace – and such a showplace. Jewelers' windows gleamed along the path with remarkable frequency. Florist shops, furriers, haberdashers, confectioners, all followed in rapid procession. The street was full of coaches. Pompous doormen, in immense coats with shiny brass belts and buttons, waited in front of expensive salesrooms . . . The whole street bore the flavor of riches and show and Carrie felt that she was not of it. She could not, for the life of her, assume the attitude and smartness of Mrs. Vance, who in her beauty was all assurance. She could only imagine that it must be evident to many that she was the less handsomely dressed of the two. It cut her to the quick, and she resolved that she would not come here again until she

looked better. At the same time, she longed to feel the delight
of parading here as an equal. Ah, then she would be happy.
(XXIV, 324)

There is the same division here between access to view and
access to possession and participation: Carrie can see but not
have, see but not "be seen" as "an equal" to her companion or
anyone else. Again, pain and desire are joined together; the
pang of exclusion goes with the wish to take part. "It cut her to
the quick," and yet, in a bizarrely exhibitionist form of the
dream of democracy, "she longed to feel the delight of parading here as an equal."

The passage points out the identification of things,
specifically clothes, with the personal status of the wearer in
others' eyes. The critical "glance" of assessment on the part of
the shopgirls withers Carrie into a consciousness of her
categorical difference from the store's legitimate customers as
an outsider, illicitly inside, having no money. Here, her best
clothes are still wanting in relation to others', and the sense of
her lack is focused in the particular comparison with Mrs Vance
as she feels that "it must be evident to many that she was the less
handsomely dressed of the two." The luxurious goods in the
windows of the various shops "followed in rapid procession,"
just like the living people in "fashion's throng." The others can
put on the things, "assume" the status which gives them the
right to walk "as an equal" in the world of fashion's making.
Carrie, "not of it," wishes to rectify the discrepancy between
her and them, her and Mrs Vance; and the question of self-
image, how she appears to others and hence to herself, is bound
up entirely with her mode of dress: "She resolved that she
would not come here again until she looked better."

Self-esteem is always material in Dreiser, and there is no
more significant indication of the progress of Carrie's career
than the details he gives of the gradual rise in her income while
Hurstwood, out of a job, wastes away his limited capital, "content to droop supinely while Carrie drifted out of his life"
(XLII, 400). Significantly, Hurstwood's continuing vigor

depends on his capacity to be the breadwinner. Whereas it was a man's money that saved Carrie when she was on the streets, Hurstwood taking over this role of provider from Drouet, the novel nowhere suggests that Carrie's earnings might continue to maintain Hurstwood's appearance. This asymmetry throws an interesting light on Veblen's point in *The Theory of the Leisure Class* that women's expensive fashions are a vicarious display of the wealth of the man who pays for them. The situation is not reversed when the woman makes money: on the contrary, the unproductive Hurstwood is a burden of which Carrie, sufficient in her own image, her own self-display, does not hesitate to free herself. Hurstwood measures his standing first of all in dollar income, of which the material evidence (including an attractive woman) is a necessary manifestation but secondary to this in importance, since what he spends has to have come from his own pocket. Lacking adequate means, he can only droop. For Carrie, on the other hand, money is only the prerequisite to a fashionable lifestyle and appearance – indispensable, but meaningless without this power of transformation into other things. In their different relations to the money and things which both regard as constitutive of their self-esteem, Carrie's rise is predicated on Hurstwood's fall. The "chasm between them" (XIII, 400) is the gap against which Carrie measures her own worth as she drifts upwards along the infinite line of success and desire, buying herself more and more clothes while Hurstwood's disintegrate into rags.

It follows *a fortiori* from this that the materially constituted self can be no more stable than the transitory images which claim the investment of its desire. In a powerful new reading of the novel,[4] Walter Benn Michaels shows how Dreiser has moved away from the fixed moral and economic order associated with classic realism:

> Where Howells identifies character with autonomy, Dreiser . . . identifies it with desire, an involvement with the world so central to one's sense of self that the distinction between what one is and what one wants tends to disappear.[5]

The limits of an older economy of scarcity and moral restraint have given way to the impersonality and boundless scale of monopoly capitalism, where responsibility is superseded by desire. This can be related to the change in orientation from production to consumption, as an ethics of work; individual enterprise gives way to the free-floating possibilities of a com-modified world. Michaels is surely right to protest against critics who have persistently seen a conscious authorial projec-tion in the soberly anti-materialistic Robert Ames, who impresses Carrie on one or two occasions and persuades her to read Balzac. The solid literary values represented by the mid-westerner are simply an anachronism.

But while it is broadly true, as Michaels says, that "*Sister Carrie* is not anti-capitalist at all,"[6] the novel does not present a world in which capitalism in its hypothetical utopian form has been achieved. Behind the attractive images of consumption, it clearly shows up some of the peculiar disparities created by that institution in the form it took in the 1890s. These are years of glamorous pleasure for those who can afford a spectacular city lifestyle,[7] but the economy of scarcity is still a daily reality for those who, like Carrie in Chicago and later on Hurstwood in New York, have no means of financial support. Given the infinite extension and desirability of what can be seen and not had, scarcity figures now as the harshness of deprivation. For those excluded, a lack of power (to buy) makes a mockery of the old realism and the old ideology grounded in the force of a moral will. There is no desire in *Sister Carrie* to turn back from the perspective of 1900, which sees and celebrates the shows of a new material prosperity. But the divisions and deprivations on which this surplus still depends appear in an even sharper focus viewed from the heights of an economy of spectacular abundance.

The mirror which makes the self into an image read and regarded by others figures clearly in the value that Carrie attaches to having her picture printed in a magazine, after she has started to make a name on Broadway: "When would some paper think her photo worthwhile?" (XLVI, 442). After the first short notice appears, Carrie has moved beyond even a position of equality on the sidewalks of affluence to become the equivalent of the superior model in the shop window. Not just a face in the crowd, "she began to think that the world was taking note of her" (XLVI, 443). But the process which copies her image thousands of times also makes Carrie an outsider in a new sense. Removed from everyday standards of comparison to the status of a star beyond reach, she becomes the high point of an image of solipsistic self-love: reading the description of herself, alone in her triumph, "Carrie hugged herself with delight" (XLVI, 443).

The making of Carrie into an image *par excellence*, a celebrity set apart for others to emulate and envy,[8] is premised upon her own conscientious reproduction of the dress and manners of women she sees about her. Carrie, "who was created with that passivity of soul which is always the mirror of the active world" (XVII, 157), is seen early on in Drouet's apartment, practising

> those little modish ways which women adopt when they would presume to be something. She looked in her mirror and pursed her lips, accompanying it with a little toss of the head as she had seen the railroad treasurer's daughter do. (XI, 104)

Satisfaction with what she sees in the glass is dependent on a third element, apart from the coupling of face and mirror image, which is that of the "modish ways" observed in other women. To be "something" means, paradoxically, to imitate passively and minutely gestures which are not her own.[9] Carrie's "personality," her recognition as an individual, is guaranteed only to the extent that it is an exact reflection of others' – in this case, that of the railroad treasurer's daughter. Carrie adapts to her world when she can "adopt" or put on wholesale the forms of behavior others suggest, down to the last shake of the head or purse of the lips.

The connection between imitation and acting, Carrie's

Ache

eventual career, is a natural one, involving no change of direction: so Carrie here rehearses her appearance before others in
the guise of the railroad treasurer's daughter. The identification
between the role-playing of the literal stage and that of
everyday life is made explicit when Carrie takes her first part as
an amateur actress and puts on the "make-up which was to
transform her, a simple maiden, to Laura, the Belle of Society"
(XIX, 176):

> She had wondered at the greatness of the names upon the
> billboards, the marvel of the long notices in the papers, the
> beauty of the dresses upon the stage – the atmosphere of car-
> riages, flowers, refinement. Here was no illusion. Here was an
> open door to all of that . . . .
>
> She could not help thinking what a delight this would be if it
> would endure, how perfect a state, if only she could do well
> now, and then sometime get a hold on her . . . . Ah! ah! to be rid
> of idleness and the drag of loneliness – to be doing and rising –
> to be admired, petted, raised to a state where all was applause,
> elegance, assumption of dignity . . . .
>
> Outside in the little lobby, another scene was being enacted.
> (XIX, 177)

Scenes are acted both inside and outside the theatre, on and off
the stage: no qualitative distinction exists, except in so far as
this inner sanctum represents the summation of all that the
world can offer, a "chamber of diamonds and delight" (XIX,
177). The stage, with all its paraphernalia of things and clothes
and newspaper celebrity, in fact consists of all the same elements that, in the world outside, go to the making (up) of a successful individual. That Carrie should want to "get a place as a
real actress" makes perfect sense if the stage is the epitome of
reality, and imitation the model for individuation.

Acting remains a real job ("to be rid of idleness . . . to be
doing"), the money it pays providing the means for the
purchase of all the goods that go to supply someone with a
recognizable identity, to make him or her "an equal" on
Broadway and in society. From one perspective, work is

oppressive, an inescapable requirement for the bare maintenance of life, as with the unemployed Carrie on her first visit
to The Fair. And the desirable objects that its earnings can buy,
being indispensable to social recognition, represent another
form of tyranny, being indispensable to the construction of a
social identity. What Dreiser stresses, however, is the positive
opportunity supplied by the two in combination: work and its
rewards of wealth and status, "doing and rising." The
Hurstwoods of the bread line and Brooklyn strikebreaking,
struggling feebly and falling, are not excluded from the picture,
but in a sense they act only as the backdrop, the bottom line or
underpaid chorus line, which sets off the "delight" of the real/
imitation world of the successful.

Sandy Petrey has recently put forward a reinterpretation of
Dreiser's much-vaunted "two styles" – the simple narrative
and the prosy moralizing which has earned him epithets like
"cloddish," "clumsy," "elephantine."[10] He argues that the
effect of the latter style is to foreground the disjunction "between social myths and social reality,"[11] exposing the valueless-
ness of the contemporary world through what is in fact a
parody, intentional or not, of the language of popular literary
sentimentalism. In Petrey's reading, the scenes in the shoe factory, at Brooklyn, and among the down-and-outs of New York
function as an abrupt thematic intrusion of reality counter-
posed to "the language of false consciousness." Much emphasis
is given to a sentence quoted above in the passage on Carrie's
stage debut: "Here was no illusion." Petrey takes this as an
ironic description of the misguidedness of Carrie's feelings at
this point: "An unequivocal sentence . . . states her impression
on entering the theatrical space which has been synonymous
with illusion since the beginning of western culture."[12]

But the theatre, according to the reading above, is not the site
of a radical contrast with the world outside it; on the contrary,
it stands at the peak of a continuum marked off at one end by
the base level of subsistence, having no means to act, and at the
other by the figure of the actor or actress, the made-up maker

of illusions. The Broadway scene, with "fashion's throng, on parade in a showplace," is as much a place of illusion and costume as the literal stage.

In the new realism that corresponds to the new consumer capitalism, "all that the individual imagines in contemplating a dazzling, alluring or disturbing spectacle" (VIII, 78) is as real as the loaf of bread for which Hurstwood stands in line. The worker in the shoe factory is governed by need, but his or her mind is still "colored" by the "spectacle," the "parade," the "display" of the things which s/he does not have, the identities s/he cannot act or put on. Image and illusion are from the start constitutive of how things appear, of what goes to make up a human subject, and of what he or she apprehends as real. "Things" are inseparable from how they look, the relative value or status they represent. The arbitrariness of commodities and exchange precedes a hypothetical stability of use and need.[13]

"All the world's a stage" takes its characteristic twentieth-century form in this novel of narcissistic consumer-actors, passively drifting up and down a line whose successive stages are marked by differences in the possession of wealth and commodities. It is the shops and not the people, the infinite displays of goods, which move "in rapid procession" down Broadway, street of the stage: things for sale take precedence over people in a strangely reified fulfillment of Shakespeare's other "mystic line, 'There are more things in heaven and earth, Horatio, than are dreamt of in your philosophy' " (VII, 78).

5

"Traffic in her desires": Zola's *Au Bonheur des Dames*

The title of Zola's novel about a Paris department store clearly alludes to the one where he carried out the bulk of his preliminary researches, whose plastic carrier bags a century later still bear the evocative legend, "Au Bon Marché."[1] "Au Bonheurs des Dames" and "Au Bon Marché": the intimate relations between "ladies' happiness" and the "good deal" or "cheap store," between what a woman wants or might want and the market forces of consumer capitalism, here stand out with all the subliminal suggestion of an advertising jingle: "Au Bon . . . Au Bon . . . Au Bon . . ."

Eve's Ransom brought out some of the complexities of late nineteenth-century representations and practices bearing on women. *Sister Carrie*, on the other hand, was less about the images constraining women than the contributions of money and what it can buy to the construction of a self-image: something both narcissistically gratifying and recognizable in society. *Au Bonheur des Dames* brings the two sides together in a single, richly symbolic modern space. Women and money; ideologies of femininity and ideologies of consumption; the image decreed and the image bought; the markings of people and prices; the selling of a society of female consumers: all are

66

related with deft precision in Zola's story. Like Dreiser's and Gissing's, it figures the arrival of an inexperienced girl in the big city, which serves as a narrative device for describing how urban consumer attractions impress themselves on a woman initially innocent of their appeal.

Michael B. Miller discusses how the traditional patriarchal structure of relations in French commerce was successfully modified and retained to fit the needs of a large-scale enterprise.[2] The old kind of small family business is exemplified in the novel by the *Vieil Elboeuf*, a fabric store owned by Denise's uncle, where for generations the current male apprentice has been *de facto* the heir to both the store and the proprietor's daughter. This pattern was successfully expanded in the Bon Marché to a *grande famille* of thousands of employees, presided over by the parental figures of Monsieur and Madame Boucicaut. This is suggested in the "paternal tone," the "genial god persona,"[3] with which Octave Mouret, the owner of *Au Bonheur des Dames*, benevolently rules his laboring subjects. The marriage of Octave and Denise at the end presents an image of bourgeois domestic harmony guiding the store like the one achieved by Aristide Boucicaut and his wife, transcending divisions of class in the symbolic union of the capitalist and the worker as man and wife.

This discussion will explore a different, though related, ideological adaptation or elision: less the selling of the new as like the old than the selling of "the new" as a value in itself. The immediate predecessors of department stores were the *magasins de nouveauté*, a species of large emporium usually specializing in fabrics for clothes, which had come into existence during the first half of the century. As the name suggests, however, the unifying criterion for its merchandise was newness, fashionability. The word says nothing about the nature or use of the goods it designates. The introduction of *nouveauté* as a value marks the transition from a commercial order based on the supplying of regular, constant demand, to one largely based on saleability: on presenting an object in a novel, desirable light irrespective of any pre-existing need. *Nouveautés*, which can be anything from a piece of lace to a model of the Arc de Triomphe, are pure commodities. They have nothing in common except the price, the fact that they can be bought in a store for money.

The fashion side of the *magasins de nouveauté* was not a new invention. But where *la mode* had previously been accessible only to the aristocracy, to those who could pay for a personal service, it was now, through the developing production of the cheaper *confections* or ready-made goods, to extend its market to the bourgeoisie. With "la démocratisation du luxe," all the trappings of fashionable modernity were in principle free for anyone to acquire, without distinction of class.[4]

One effect of an image of classlessness is to leave the individual as the only significant social category. Rather than someone known to everyone, and knowing a settled place in a finite community, he or she becomes just a face in the crowd, with the averageness of a statistic when viewed from outside it. From within, identity – be it "standing out" or "blending in" – is visually established. This reinforces the tendency of marketing techniques to focus their attention on the adornment of the individual body as that which is outwardly visible. To this extent, the person selecting clothes that will fit – conventional enough to conform but distinctive enough to show individuality, to look a bit different – is in a sense a type of derivative entrepreneur, selling an image of him- or herself to an unknown, generalized audience. Individuation, in the form of a modern self-image, is inseparable from appearance. The spectacle of the department-store experience, with its show of merchandise and palatial buildings, typifies this theatrical effect.

Rosalind H. Williams has written a stimulating study of the early history of consumer ideology in France, especially contemporary debates about "the democratization of luxury."[5] In the wake of the countercultural movement of the 1960s and the economic realism of the 1970s, Williams argues, through her interpretation of the decisive period a century ago, for a median level of rational consumption: between the reified and the primitive, or between excess and complete renunciation. She seeks to replace the individualistic, atomizing tendencies of consumer culture by a notion of "solidarist austerity" and suggests that "our moral task is to distinguish valid pleasures and uses of commodities from trivial and inauthentic ones."[6] But such formulations can only appear more or less arbitrary, precisely because of the very transformation of commerce which she identifies as a turning-point. When the criterion of stable demand in determining what is made and sold and bought is replaced simply by that of the product's capacity to be perceived as desirable (and hence sold), there is no way of defining some more "reasonable" state of affairs on a smaller scale. What might have been taken as an average or basic standard of living say eighty years ago would clearly be radically different from today's equivalent: we are now at an even more "advanced" – materially encumbered or supplied – stage of consumer capitalism. The "dream worlds" in the space of the store and the fantasies of the mind are neither "real" nor "illusory" in any absolute sense, and the meaning attached to both terms shifts along with varying economic determinations of "reasonable" and "desirable" standards of living. What is interesting and promising in Williams's proposals is the notion of collective consumption, and her reference to the demands of Third-World countries, whose systematic exploitation and relative lack of access to the consumer goods they produce parallels working-class exploitation in the nineteenth century.

In Zola's novel, Octave Mouret has ambitions that bow to no concepts of prudent moderation or tradition, as the store's profits increase by geometric leaps and bounds in the several years covered by the novel.[7] His intention, repeated often, to "révolutionner Paris," equated with the specific project to "révolutionner le commerce des nouveautés" (I, 43), recalls the contemporary maxim of "la démocratisation du luxe." But this is decidedly a revolution from the top, an imperialistic transformation on the part of a ruling class, extending from the projects of real estate purchase and building in Paris itself, to the colonialist manoeuvres of sending out thousands of catalogues to the provinces, and indeed to the farthest limits of the French-speaking world.[8]

If, on the other hand, the world outside will be radically altered by the appearance of the *Bonheur des Dames*, visibly advertising its presence by the painted delivery vans and billboard posters all over Paris, and the catalogues bearing its name, the store itself is also a model in miniature of an entirely new form of existence. It represents, to begin with, a literal inversion or mutation of nature, displaying its simulated seasons in new collections months before the intended season of fall or spring comes round. The following passage describes the sensations of Mme. Marty and Mme. de Boves, two of the bourgeois ladies who frequent the store, when they enter it on the opening day of one of Mouret's big sales:

> A sense of well-being spread through them, they felt they were entering into spring on leaving the winter of the street. While outside the wind blew, frozen with hailstones, within the halls of the *Bonheur* there was already the mild warmth of the beautiful season with the light fabrics, the floral brightness of the colors, the rustic gaiety of the summer fashions and the sun-shades. (IX, 264-5)[9]

The diffuse "well-being" invading them fulfills the rubric implied by the name of the store through feelings well calculated by the manager of the affair. It is a colonization of the mind designed to produce new areas of need and desire, new relations to things and to nature, corresponding to the different departments of the store and the *nouveautés* which they sell.

Mouret states clearly to Baron Hartmann the effects of the *grands magasins* upon *la femme*:

> They had aroused new bodily desires in her, they were a huge temptation to which she was doomed to succumb, yielding first of all to the purchases of a prudent housewife, then won over by the coquettish things, then consumed. (III, 110)[10]

As the *Bonheur* grows in size, Octave invents new categorizations of ever more detailed application, suggesting the purchase of separate items for different ages, sizes and parts of the body, different occasions or times of the day – "de lôngs vêtements blancs, libres et minces, où l'on sentait l'étirement des matinées paresseuses, au lendemain des soirs de tendresse" (long white garments, loose and slender, where you sensed the stretching out of lazy mornings following evenings of love) (XIV, 421) – with all the particularized elements of what is today called "lifestyle."

At first sight, this expansion of choices and available goods, free to be seen and pondered by anyone entering the store or passing its alluring *vitrines*, does represent a model of egalitarian modernity. The art gallery and reading room, the refreshments and other amenities available to the clientele, make it also a place where women can actually pass the whole day, experiencing a form of the luxurious new life that is being sold to them:

> Women came to spend their vacant hours at his place, the thrilling and anxious hours they used to pass in the depths of chapels: necessary expenditure of nervous emotion, revived struggle of a god countering the husband, endlessly renewed cult of the body, with the divine hereafter of Beauty. (XIV, 437)[11]

"Elles sont chez elles," "they are at home," as Mouret smugly puts it (IX, 271); but only to the extent that they are also "chez lui," "at his place." The stroke of genius is to build a "firmament du rêve" (XIV, 437) which has the aura of enfranchisement, of freedom from husbands and conventional restraints, but is in fact simply a functional equivalent of the Church, filling the woman's hours of *ennui* with a place to worship, experience ecstasy, spend her "passion nerveuse" and her money. The "cathédrale du commerce moderne" (IX, 258) is thus uniquely favored by the gods and the market, fitting in both with the new ideology of modernity and with existing feminine needs for somewhere to pass the time and dream under a "god countering the husband," an alternative male authority.

The double movement of limitless fantasies supported by strategic, rational planning is figured in the description of Mouret's mistress, Mme. Desforges, surveying the scene on one of the big sale days and "seized by the passionate vitality animating the great nave that day":

> Mirrors everywhere extended the shop space, reflecting displays with corners of the public, faces the wrong way round, halves of shoulders and arms. (IX, 272)[12]

In the boundless, and carefully planned, extension of mirror reflections, multiplying the desires of the gazer and the displays of things, the people present are marginalized into "corners of the public," broken up into warped or divided body parts ("faces the wrong way round, halves of shoulders and arms"). They are bare objects without connection, which recover a semblance of unity not in relation to a whole human body or a collective group, but only as part of the colorful commodity images by which Mme. Desforges is "seized," according to Mouret's design.

In another description of women looking at endless arrays of *tissus*, a different side of this peculiarly modern gaze of desire and fascination shows through:

> And below, as in a basin, slumbered the heavy fabrics, the special weaves, the damasks, the brocades, the beaded and lamé silks, amidst a deep bed of velvet, all the velvets, black, white, colored, interwoven with silk or satin, scooping out with their shifting marks a motionless lake on which reflections of sky and landscape seemed to dance. Women, pale with desire, leaned over as if to see themselves. All of them, confronted by this discharged waterfall, remained standing, secretly fearing they would be captivated by such overwhelming luxury, and unable to resist the longing to throw themselves in and be lost in it. (IV, 136)[13]

The outdoor nature of landscape, lake and sky is brought inside to form the spectacle of the sleeping new material world which attracts the lookers.[14] A total loss of control is produced by these "étoffes," truly the stuff that consumer dreams are made of: "pale with desire," the women are caught in an ambivalent weaving together of fear and longing, "peur" and "envie"; they are compelled at once to a grasp of appropriation ("s'y jeter") and a loss of self or self-possession ("s'y perdre"), an irretrievable fall of the moral mind into the midst of an infinite expanse of substantial things. The "deep bed" and "discharged waterfall" seduce the women into their irresistible wish for a spectacular *consommation*.[15] Together and equal they stand as Narcissi before their "motionless lake" of consumer goods which possesses and holds them by the allure of the possessions it offers them, and consumes them in the same moment which fabricates their desires as those of consumers. There is no certainty of perspective in this passive exchange between women and the things in front of their eyes.

One evening Denise, the novel's heroine, and one more provincial arrival in the big city, is "attracted once more" by the store's *vitrines*. What she sees behind the glass, however, is "the curved profile of a woman with no head" (I, 65). Like these models of what they desire or desire to be, the women who stare in wonder have lost their heads. Wanting to make themselves one with the mindless, topless image, they are objectified – and objectify themselves – into mere bodies, potential bearers of clothes. "As if to see themselves," they lean over to find not themselves, but the things which would make each one *fit* to be seen, the *total* woman.

Parallel to this fragmentation and objectification of women identified and identifying with dressed-up bodies and body parts, is the division of life and its materials into ever more minutely specified areas of attention, which are represented by the various departments or *rayons* of the *grand magasin* and the goods which they offer for sale. The agency of Mouret, whose stature grows with the takings of his enterprise and its own increasing control over the life of Paris and of the women who buy, is common to both developments. Mouret is at once "master of the conquered city" (III, 105) through his store, and self-styled seducer in the "love market," the "marché d'amour" (X, 290), where Denise is the only one of his chosen shop-girls who refuses to comply. Mouret's attitude in the conquest of women, whether personally or through the shopping medium, is made up of a combination of reverence and hatred, in which the first is a means to the sadistic achievement of the second:

> Mouret's sole wish was to conquer Woman. He wanted her to be queen in his establishment; he had built her this temple to hold her at his mercy there. This was his whole strategy, to intoxicate her with gallant consideration and traffic in her desires, exploit her excitement. So he racked his brains night and day in search of inventive new ideas. (IX, 258)[16]

Mouret's "sole passion," split into two directly opposite channels of expression, is no more simply or naturally given than the diverse, diverted desires of the women he holds "at his mercy" through the laboriously constructed spectacles and devices of his "inventive new ideas." But in practice, it works like a dream. Love and hate, submission and exploitation, religion and capital, find themselves in perfect accord in this giant new invention of the modern department store.

Zola's novels are always based on extensive research of the milieu, and a striking linguistic parallel here with a recorded speech of the historical equivalent of Mouret draws attention to the fidelity of his account. Just before the grand opening of the new Bon Marché buildings in 1872, Boucicaut took a sudden decision to rearrange all the departments, which he justified as follows:

> What's necessary . . . is that they walk around for hours, that they get lost. First of all, they will seem more numerous. Secondly . . . the store will seem larger to them. And lastly, it would really be too much if, as they wander around in this organized disorder, lost, driven crazy, they don't set foot in

some departments where they had no intention of going, and if
they don't succumb at the sight of things which grab them on
the way.[17]

There is no question here of the "rational" consumer. Rather,
Boucicaut explicitly announces his aim to make his female
clientele "lost, driven crazy," as in Zola's "seduced, driven
crazy" (II, 76). He intends them to be diverted into departments they had no intention of visiting to be deprived of all
planning capacity by the master plan which controls their confusion. "This organized disorder" thus applies not only to the
literal space of the store, but to the minds of its feminine customers. "Choice," in the utilitarians' sense of rational decision-
making, has no relevance to them, though it is what governs the
patron's strategy. Succumbing to its calculated effect depends,
in fact, on their losing their reason, going mad.

Jesus threw the merchants out of the temple in Jerusalem;
nineteen hundred years on, church and market happily coexist
in the "cathedral of modern commerce," with priest and seller
united in the single person of Mouret, the "amiable god" (II,
80). And there are more religious associations engaged in this
rise or raising of a new commercial world, which turns out to
be in one sense a resurrection after death. The recurring dialec-
tic in Zola's novels between stagnation and fecundity, death
and rebirth, "death for continual sowing" (XIV, 402), here
takes the form of a replacement of the outworn, outdated
"dead shop windows" (II, 87) of the small local store by the
showy vitality of the new.

There is an even more direct indication of death, figured first
in the ghostly presence of Octave's former wife, "this dead
woman in the foundations" (II, 87) and then in the martyrdom
of Denise's aunt and cousin at the *Vieil Elbeuf*. That all three
are women is no accident. "The slow agony of Geneviève," the
cousin (VIII, 234), involves a physical "consumption," a bodily
return to childhood and loss of femininity, brought about by
the attraction of her fiancé, Columban, to one of the *demoiselles*

of the *Bonheur des Dames*. Having none of the allures of modern dress or the *bonheur* of Mouret's women, Geneviève is reduced to a state of "wretched nudity" when she speaks to Denise from her deathbed:

> It was the end of the flesh, a fiancée's body used up in waiting, returned to infancy, as slender as in the first years. Slowly, Geneviève covered herself over again and repeated, "You see, I'm no longer a woman." (XIII, 381)[18]

Behind the facade of Mouret's "dream palace" (IX, 271) in honor and exploitation of a new woman, rests the defenseless, emaciated body of a bygone type of femininity, her body "used up" in its very virginity, its separation from the modern forms of female sexuality.

The reduction of women to dead bodies is only the reverse side of their reduction to, and celebration as, sexual bodies in the new order of things. But other kinds of physical agony are exacted in the unseen foundations of the new store: the rigors of the thirteen-hour day required of the workers, who eat in the basement, in some cases live in the attic, and perform their duties as unobtrusively as possible.[19] Their part in Mouret's revolution requires not so much the formation of a new type of gendered subjectivity as a complete suppression of the structures of difference acted out and produced in the world of the clientele. It is their mundane work behind the scenes which is the hidden basis for the spectacle in which the customers are invited to participate.

This reverse side of the dream of democratic luxury shows a mechanical parody of equality, with the individual becoming simply a numerical unit, quantitatively identical to every other worker. When Denise presents herself for employment, she is immediately reduced in name to the faceless "number 7" (IV, 21). But Mouret's "factory" or "machine"[20] is so skilfully managed that it includes a commission system, *la gueulte*, designed to set each of the units against the others, vying for extra pay in their common subjection:

[This mechanism] created a struggle for survival among the staff from which the boss profited. In his hands, moreover, this struggle became the favorite device, the organizational principle he constantly applied. He released emotions, brought anger out in the open, let the big ones eat the little ones, and grow fat on this battle of interests. (II, 72)[21]

Other strategies, such as the hierarchies within each department and the ruthless firings that take place annually during the aptly named "dead season" reinforce the brutal efficiency of this modern mechanism. For this sector of his enterprise, Mouret creates a Darwinian world without illusions, where the big beasts eat the little ones and fraternization is discouraged to the point of a rule forbidding one *demoiselle* to enter another's room.

Whereas the image of the store as a "dream palace" relies on its seductive projection of a commodified sexuality, the equally mediated, non-natural jungle behind the counter subsists in the loss of the sexual and social identities current in the world outside. To the customers, the staff are beneath consideration and do not appear as gendered individuals: "He was not a man, she used him for intimate services with her customary disdain for people in her employment, without even looking at him" (IV, 133). But the same is true for the relations between *vendeurs* themselves, with only the difference that contempt is replaced by rivalry:

If the continual battle over money had not effaced the sexes, the constant jostling would have been enough to kill desire.... They were all of them mere wheels, finding themselves carried along by the drive of the machine, laying aside their personalities and simply contributing their powers. (V, 164)[22]

As cogs in the machine, the assistants suffer the effacement of both sex and personality. The salesgirls are also rendered neutral, persons apart, in another way, which is the indeterminacy of their social status:

The worst of it was their neutral, indeterminate position between the lady and the shop assistant. Cast like this into the midst of luxury, often without previous instruction, they constituted a separate class without name. (XI, 330)[23]

This classless, sexless, nameless collection of numbered bodies is the supporting mechanism and the suppressed antithesis of the fabulous world of *Au Bonheur des Dames*. Arriving for tea with Mme. Desforges, the Baron Hartmann notices Denise patiently waiting and casually inquires:

"Who is it?"
"Oh – no-one," replied Mme. Desforges in her nasty voice.
"A store girl who's waiting." (XI, 329)[24]

Mouret's dream factory thus operates at two distinct but inter-dependent levels, producing two diametrically opposite functional places for woman, at once a sexless producer and a sexual god-dess celebrated in the "temple built for the cult of her body" (IX, 276). This contradiction is represented in the figure of Denise, who moves upwards from being a sales assistant at the lowest level to become the equal of any bourgeois consumer as Mouret's wife. She is the symbolic "unknown queen" frequently heralded by the narrative as the future avenger of his high-handed autocracy. The novel's last word commends the humanitarian reforms in the workers' conditions achieved through the influence of this "omnipotent" Denise (XIV, 442). But though she holds out for a higher price than any woman before her, Denise capitulates in just the same way to Mouret's ultimately irresistible offers. "Omnipotent" in appearance, her power in fact extends only to modifications of the existing sys-tem. Like Mme. Bourdelais, type of the rational consumer or "smart shopper," who profits from all the loss leaders[25] and free facilities of the store without getting carried away, Denise stands for the strong version of the woman in consumer society, prac-tically adept within the available limits. But she cannot begin to erase or change the ambivalent aspects of being a woman in that society – what she experiences as "these contradictions of her being, where she ceased to read clearly" (X, 321).

The lack of place and the mental confusion of women within the store is explicitly described as a male project, not only on the part of Mouret but via his financial alliance with the Baron Hartmann. But it is significant that this connection is brought about through the mediation, requested by Octave, of Mme. Desforges, currently his mistress and formerly Hartmann's. Thus is established "a link between the baron and himself, so tight between men of gallant nature" (III, 105). Women are not a definite subject with a given nature or essence, but rather a "link," a relational instrument utilized between the solid agencies of men:

> And with a few sentences spoken in Baron Hartmann's ear, as if he had made the sort of amorous confidences that are sometimes hazarded between men, [Octave] finished explaining the mechanism of modern large-scale commerce. Higher on the list than the facts so far given appeared the exploitation of women. It was over women that the stores were fighting their competitive battles, it was women they caught in the endless trap of their cheap sales, after dazing them in front of their displays. (III, 110)[26]

Behind the gallantry displayed in the outward honor of women, Mouret whispers that the meaning of true love is a sexual and financial partnership of men, a union of masculine interests based on the manipulation of women: "a sudden embrace between these men who had engaged in so many joint commercial battles" (XIV, 415).

Mouret's enterprise invents or inflects many types and relationships of female subjectivity, ranging from the unsexed, unclassed *ouvrière* to the glorified narcissistic body draped in all the commodified wonder of "costly fantasies" (XIV, 422).[27] But the formal resolution at the end of the novel in the marriage of Octave and Denise appeals to a more traditional notion of "l'éternel féminin" (XIV, 415). The sympathy Denise feels for her fellow workers and for the old-fashioned *petits commerçants* deprived of their livelihood is said to originate in "her woman's soul" (XIII, 402), modifying and assuaging the harsher effects of the work of Mouret, who "had invented this mechanism for crushing the world" (XIII, 402).

The relation of masculine and feminine here is one of ideological complementarity, "the feminine" being a timeless quality presumably shared in some degree by all women with souls, just as the masculinity it counterbalances would be an irreducible quality of men. In this connection, a number of other pairings come to light. Zola's language repeatedly draws attention to the difference between the machine and the dream, the profit-making business superintended by masculine rationality and the fantasy world it constructs in the form of the feminine "temple of luxury." That the two are in practice hierarchically structured and mutually interdependent is clear enough; but even the formal distinction breaks down.

Mouret's plans for the future of the *Bonheur des Dames* partake of more than cold calculation. When he first acquires the store, "he was already imagining it with a palatial facade, commanding, master of the conquered city" (III, 105), a dream of domination in one sense as wild as the abandonment he creates and inspires in his clientele. Baron Hartmann at first considers the lack of evident realism in Mouret's idea the mark of a "poet"; "What imagination!" is his amazed response. But the same non-rational quality is also Mouret's "commercial genius" (III, 107), as subsequent successes abundantly demonstrate.

From the other side, the window-shopper is drawn to look by forces that have little to do with imagination. Newly arrived in the city, Denise and her brothers find themselves in front of

---

Illustration 7   Shopping in Regent Street, 1890: "*Shopping* is checking out the stores – for ladies; for gentlemen, it's checking out the *lady shoppers*! *Shop* qui peut!"

Shopping was an occasion to see and be seen, and department store reading rooms were notorious as venues for illicit rendezvous between the sex which shopped for things and the sex which shopped for women.

SHOPPING DANS REGENT STREET

    Shopping, c'est courir les magasins : voilà pour
les dames ; mais pour les messieurs, c'est courre
les *shoppingeuses ! Shop* qui peut !

the imposing new *grand magasin*: "mechanically they took the rue Neuve-Saint-Augustin and followed the shop windows, stopping once more in front of each display" (I, 43). This mechanical allure, the rational compulsion of fantasy, is only the obverse of the fantastic reason which produces it.

The confusion is brought out again by a description of a scene in the store on another of its big sale days which describes the "amazing motion of the afternoon, when the overheated machine led the dance of the clients and took money from their flesh" (IV, 140). Here, the frightening movement is made up of mechanical dances and moneyed female bodies, or dancing machines and sexual money – elements entirely welded together in this climax of the ambivalent life of *Au Bonheur des Dames*. "Jeu calculé," a "contrived game," like Boucicaut's "désordre organisé," it is itself a model for the attractive and confusing modes of existence in consumer society which it shows to its clients and imposes on its workers. Dream and machine come together in the spectacular displays of *Au Bonheur* as Mouret, who "was only doing the work of his era" (XIII, 389), changes the face of things and the workings of human minds, with all the strange powers and charisma of a "despot" (XIV, 437) keeping his subjects under an illusion of freedom.

Zola wrote down in his preliminary sketch that the book would be "le poème de la vie moderne."[28] There is as much ambiguity in that phrase as there is in the novel he eventually wrote about the transformation of commerce. At the end, the store dedicated to trafficking in new desires for women takes its first million in a day, while its owner marries himself to "the eternal feminine" in the form of his virgin bride. Such is the enigmatic interest – the poetic profit – of the shopkeeper's counter revolution.

6

Culture and
the book business

The commercial revolution of the nineteenth century turned all things beneath its touch into glittering commodities, including some which might at first sight seem unlikely candidates. In W.D. Howells' essay on "The art of the adsmith," the imaginary dialogue contains the following passage:

"Ad is a loathly little word, but we must come to it. It's as legitimate as lunch. But as I was saying, the adsmith seems to have caught the American business tone, as perfectly as any of our novelists have caught the American social tone."

"Yes," said my friend, "and he seems to have prospered as richly by it. You know some of those chaps make fifteen or twenty thousand dollars by adsmithing. They have put their art quite on a level with fiction pecuniarily."

"Perhaps it *is* a branch of fiction."

"No; they claim that it is pure fact. My author discourages the slightest admixture of fable. The truth, clearly and simply expressed, is the best in an ad."

"It is best in a wof, too. I am always saying that."

"Wof?"

"Well, work of fiction. It's another new word, like lunch or ad."

"But in a wof," said my friend, instantly adopting it, "my author insinuates that the fashion of payments tempts you to verbosity, while in an ad the conditions oblige you to the greatest possible succinctness. In one case you are paid by the word; in the other you pay by the word."[1]

The sacred Word has become an object manufactured and sold like anything else. And far from there being any distinction between the commercial manufacturer of persuasive words and the immortal creator of artistic ones, Howells' conversation implies that the difference, if it exists, is the other way around. Fiction writers have priority in the field in terms of their inflated verbal earnings; adsmiths can only "put their art . . . on a level with fiction pecuniarily." As regards the issue of quality versus quantity, the last paragraph makes it clear that there is another unexpected reversal. Quality, in the effective "succinctness" of single words and phrases, is the adsmith's department, while the writer of "wofs" must simply keep up as rapid and substantial a production of "verbosity" as he is able.

The coinage of new words like "ad" or "lunch" is symptomatic of the prevalent conversion of words into various forms of commercially viable currency. Advertising and fiction might work closely together, as Howells suggests, by their respective capturing of America's "business" and "social" tones, but there was another more material and obvious way in which their messages were linked at the time. From the middle of the nineteenth century onwards, novels had often been published first in serialized form, either as part of another publication – magazine, newspaper, review – or in "numbers" sold separately. In both cases, they would be physically surrounded by advertisements; and these would also form part of the cheap reprint editions which increased in number and frequency during the period.[2] Novels and advertisements were therefore components of the same product: in French newspapers, to take the most extreme case, the *feuilleton* section where the novel was printed was situated at the bottom of the very same pages on which the news and advertisements appeared.

This question of the relationship between literature and commerce was summarized by the critic Sainte-Beuve in an article of 1839 already entitled "De la littérature industrielle":

> We would have had our work cut out to try in the paper to separate what remained conscientious and free-spirited from what was becoming public and mercenary . . . . How could one condemn something an inch or two away, how could one call something odious and infernal which was proclaimed and displayed as the marvel of the age an inch or two lower down? The attraction of the giant lettering of the advertisement prevailed: it was a magnetic mountain which made the compass lie.[3]

Sainte-Beuve is speaking here not of novels themselves, but of reviews juxtaposed with advertisements for books which they cannot in this (literal) context condemn. But this only reinforces the point: books themselves have become commodities promoted by their sellers like any other modern article, and their values must not undermine those of the *annonces* which appear alongside or above them. Juxtaposition tempers contradiction: without advertisements, books and journals could not be financed, and it is their commercial character which determines the general tone.

Lough, Sutherland and Tebbel give details of the technological and social changes which brought about the increasing participation of novels, and of art and literature in general, in the commercial side of nineteenth-century life. The mechanization of printing and typesetting processes and the vast reduction in the cost of paper production were the enabling conditions for the development of mass-circulation newspapers and magazines, as well as of the serial publications containing exclusively parts of unpublished novels. American publishers produced cheap editions of complete books, as in the dime novels of the second half of the century; Charpentier initiated the same kind of cut-price selling in France from 1858. In Britain the practice was slower to develop because of the habitual use of libraries: books were borrowed rather than bought, so there was no immediate incentive for publishers to apply principles of cost-effective production and so detract from the high-profit sales to libraries, who were the chief purchasers. But by the turn of the century, the increasing success of compact, inexpensive re-prints of the three-volume first editions had effected a parallel shift to those of the other two countries. Book production was becoming a modern, rationally organized industry.[4]

The complex repercussions of changes in transport may serve as a bridge between the economic and the social factors relating to the growth of the literature industry. Bradsher asserts that the introduction of steam-powered ships on the transatlantic route was the immediate cause of the marketing of serial re-prints of British novels to the United States after 1838, long before the complications of an International Copyright Law.[5] On a less global level, the construction of the European railroads from the middle of the century onwards increased both the speed and the extension of distribution facilities, so that journals and books printed in the capital could profit from markets much further afield, and a circulating library like Mudie's could function efficiently in conveying its books from London to the entire country. The greater physical size of the United States rendered such centralized operations impracticable, and this is part of the reason why publishers there experimented more with lightweight, low-cost editions, often sold by traveling salesmen rather than by booksellers with fixed premises.

If new forms of transport contributed to changes in the production and distribution of books, they were also significant in the emergence of new social conditions for the consumption of

---

Illustration 8 Both sides of the "news": the sexual division of reading reproduces the separation which sends him to the office and "serious" matters, her to the store and its trivial "novelties".

   Him: I only enjoy the paper at the office; on Sundays it's a bore to read!

   Her: Well, I only get the most interesting news on that day!

A CHACUN SON POINT DE VUE

MONSIEUR. — Le journal ne m'amuse qu'au bureau; le dimanche, sa lecture m'assomme !
MADAME. — Eh bien, moi, c'est seulement ce jour-là que j'y trouve les plus intéressantes nouvelles !

literature: the industry was affected by the passenger as well as the freight side of the new lines of communication. Unlike its more bumpy precursors, the railway journey was a relatively comfortable experience. It offered a limited period of free time ideally suited to the reading of a novel, preferably in the form of a personal copy rather than a cumbersome library edition. The market for cheap railway novels thus ultimately worked against the three-decker, in that it favored a shorter, cheaper and (in both senses) lighter product. It was a profitable line, and much importance was attached at the time to the awarding of the British franchise for station bookstalls in 1848, to the firm of W.H. Smith.

New and faster transport thus accelerated changes in the marketing of printed matter and in the sociology of reading. Its significance is a good gauge of the extent to which literature, far from remaining within a tradition of durable, leather-bound volumes, was becoming a matter of high-speed turnover and novelty, of up-to-dateness and temporary distraction. The expansion of elementary education and the parallel increase in literacy in all three countries meant a huge rise in the number of potential readers, and produced for the first time a working-class market for newspapers and books. Cheapness was crucial to those on a limited wage, and this was an incentive to the cutting of publication costs through mechanization and the inclusion of advertising material. From the publishers' side, the larger scale and increased turnover of production aimed at the new types of audience were a means to ultimately much higher profits. Some indication of the scope of these changes may be gathered from the case of newspapers. In the early part of the century, the two leading Paris dailies had circulations of around twenty thousand; by 1900, no less than four popular papers were selling a million or more.[6]

The railway novel is one example of the ways in which reading could come to supply an occupation for vacant hours. To some extent, owing to reductions in the length of the working day, this was a consideration in the publication of literature aimed at working-class readers. But large expanses of leisure time were more an attribute of the middle classes, until this time the chief consumers of marketed written material. During the course of the century their numbers, like those of the literate working class, rose rapidly, so that the reading public was expanded at this level too. Those with the largest amount of time to spare were middle-class women, staying at home but with servants carrying out the domestic work. In literature, then, as in other areas, women were the principal consumers of a product put out in most cases by men, and this has interesting results in terms of the types of argument used to defend or attack certain kinds of writing or the validity of readers' tastes. The complexity and interest of the question is clear from the way that women writers (Eliot, Sand, the Brontës, for instance) often considered it prudent to adopt a male pseudonym in approaching a publisher with a work that would be read by more women than men.[7] Women were meant to be consumers not producers, and in so far as it was a job of work and a sphere of masculine achievement, the profession of writer was unwomanly and a woman attempting to enter it was naturally at a disadvantage. But inasmuch as writing was perceived as an odd profession – because it often lacked consistent rewards of status and money and because it included some socially eccentric practitioners – it could also be taken as unmanly, suggesting the incapacity to hold down a normal job. The process of producing a manuscript was itself peculiar by comparison with most other professional and manual forms of employment at the time, in that it was usually carried on at home. But for women, it was precisely this that made writing a possibility. Domestic scribbling was an acceptable ladylike occupation; conflicts of identity only began at the point of selling a script and thereby seeking improperly to make both money and a name. A man's name – a "pen name" – could be a cover for that unfeminine thing, a published book (as well as a means of avoiding critical prejudice). For men the problem was not that they might earn money but that they might not, since income for the individual writer was in most cases unpredictable.

If word-making in general, with sophisticated methods of printing and distribution and a vastly expanded market of potential readers, was becoming a modern commercial enterprise, the initial process of composition was closer to older models of artisanal production. But the larger changes necessarily impinged upon the place of writing and writers in society. The great increase in the quantity of printed matter produced obviously brought with it a corresponding rise in the number of people employed in writing it. And just as books and journals were being incorporated into the world of competitive selling, so "men of letters" ceased in the main to be gentlemanly dilettantes, and formed a new class of professional writers entering into financial contracts with the publishers and editors who wanted to print their work. The formation of organizations for the protection and promotion of writers' interests – the *Société des gens de lettres* in France (1838) and the Society of Authors in Britain (1884) – bears witness to this development.[8]

This virtual unionization of literary producers suggests that in one sense they could be identified as members of the working class, paid according to the volume of words set down, as Howells's interlocutor implies. In another essay, "The man of letters as a man of business," Howells makes this connection explicit: "Economically, [artists] are the same as mechanics, farmers, day-laborers."[9] Anthony Trollope makes a similar point in his posthumously published *Autobiography:*

> I had long since convinced myself that in such work as mine the great secret consisted in acknowledging myself to be bound by rules of labour similar to those which an artizan or a mechanic is forced to obey.[10]

The same commitment to regular output is reflected in Zola's famous motto, *"nulla dies sine linea,"* "no day without a line," inscribed like a self-imposed shop steward over his desk at Médan.

But if writing was a job of work like any other, it must entail that the author have no personal stake in the nature or use of the product. This was a consequence which Trollope, for one, was perfectly willing to accept on behalf of his fellow "literary labourers":[11]

> I feel, with regard to literature, somewhat as I suppose an upholsterer or undertaker feels when he is called upon to supply a funeral. He has to supply it, however distasteful it may be. It is his business, and he will starve if he neglect it. So I have felt that, when anything in the shape of a novel was required, I was bound to produce it.[12]

Trollope's comfortable capitulation to market demands is paralleled in Howells' more brashly entrepreneurial "man of business":

> There is no . . . positive and obvious necessity, I am sorry to say, for fiction, or not for the higher sort of fiction. The sort of fiction which corresponds in literature to the circus and the variety theatre in the show-business seems essential to the spiritual health of the masses, but the most cultivated of the classes can get on, from time to time, without an artistic novel . . . The only thing that gives [a] writer positive value is his acceptance with the reader; but his acceptance is from month to month wholly uncertain. Authors are largely matters of fashion, like this style of bonnet, or that shape of gown. Last spring the dresses were all made with lace berthas, and Smith was read; this year the butterfly capes are worn, and Jones is the favorite author. Who shall forecast the fall and winter modes?[13]

The vacillation here is characteristic of the essay and raises a number of interesting issues. On the one hand, books are not said to be necessities, but luxury commodities to whose varying forms the successful writer must try to conform. His only "positive value is his acceptance with the reader"; yet there are clearly two distinct groups of readers – "the masses" and "the most cultivated of the classes" – with correspondingly different types of reading material. To the first, this is in fact "essential" to their "spiritual health"; for those able to "get on, from time to time, without an artistic novel," fiction is dispensable. This

makes "the higher sort of fiction," unnecessary and unpredictable in its success, logically equivalent to butterfly capes, as
compared with the stable demand for fictional equivalents of
the circus.

The equivocation in the concept of "value" – need or luxury, absolute or monetary – increases in the light of Howells'
earlier appeal to "the instinctive sense of the dishonor which
money-purchase does to art."[14] At this point in the essay, he is
making a case for the complete separation of artistic from
money-making work:

> I do not think any man ought to live by an art. A man's art
> should be his privilege, when he has proven his fitness to exer-
> cize it, and has otherwise earned his daily bread; and its results
> should be free to all.[15]

Similar assumptions lie behind Coleridge's emphatic injunction at an earlier stage of the commercialization of art to pros-
pective young writers: "NEVER PURSUE LITERATURE AS A
TRADE."[16] Art should not be inhibited or contaminated by
association with the male writer's need to earn a living amid
what Howells calls "the grotesque confusion of our economic
being."[17] In practice, this coupling of literature with a regular
job was a *modus vivendi* that many nineteenth-century writers
adopted, preferably in a situation which left them plenty of free
time for their literary endeavors. Americans were often consuls
abroad; the French establishment was usually generous in supplying sinecures or pensions to ailing *literati* when they needed
them. Coleridge's ideal occupation for this purpose was that of
a country clergyman, while Trollope, who claimed that "few
men, I think, ever lived a fuller life,"[18] was a dedicated
employee of the Post Office.

For Trollope, this choice was not a matter of financial need
(he was making a more than gentlemanly income in each of his
two professions), but neither was it the result of regarding his
literary labors as qualitatively distinct from the others. When
he speaks of his "love of letters,"[19] he means the kind that the

postman delivers, and he is vehemently opposed to the view that the writer is someone whose work cannot be subjected to the norms of regular production that operate in other fields:

> A writer . . . imagines . . . that he, as a brain-worker, and conscious of the subtle nature of the brain, should be able to exempt himself from bonds when it suits him. He has his own theory about inspiration which will not always come, – especially will not come if wine-cups overnight have been too deep. All this has ever been odious to me, as being unmanly.[20]

At its most extreme, the exaltation of art as an absolute, outside quotidian existence, might take the form of an assertion that the artist should take no part at all in daily life or work. Thus Alfred de Vigny's Chatterton:

> He needs to *do nothing* in order to do something with his art. He must do nothing useful or routine, so as to have the time to listen to the harmonies forming slowly in his soul, which the crude noise of definite, regular work interrupts and inevitably causes to fade away. This is THE POET.[21]

This solution would be one supported by Howells's divorce of artists and works of art from "the grotesque confusion of our economic being" evident in modern life. But the confusion is only compounded by his subsequent statement that "at present business is the only human solidarity."[22] No wonder then, perhaps, that there should be "no . . . positive and obvious necessity for the higher sort of fiction." Howells' "Muse" is of the type despised by Trollope, afflicting the author with unpredictable "times and seasons when he cannot blossom."[23] But that is a problem not because it inhibits the creation of genuine art, but because "these drawbacks reduce the earning capacity of what I may call the high-cost man of letters."[24] Business is the frame of reference, the first principle, and it is only in its terms – financial or logical – that the anomalous qualities of "higher" art can be proposed.

If quality shows up only as the other side of a monetary coin of "earning capacity," it is worth recalling that in the distinction between the adsmith and the novelist it was the adsmith who appeared as the producer of quality goods, of words whose worth would be measured by their "succinctness" and not by the volume of output. Apparently, however, there exists the exceptional novelist who produces "the higher sort of fiction"; and it is he, the "high-cost man of letters" paid according to a special standard, who corresponds within the novel-writing class to the adsmith or the manufacturer of butterfly capes: to those whose success is related to the arbitrary, unquantifiable values of fashion. Quality is not immortal, but the stuff of transient social tastes; it is measured not by detachment from the money-making world, but by its capacity to command a blockbuster price outside the normal scales.

This element of risk in the artistic novelist's work reinforces the connection to the entrepreneurial class implied by his identification with the adsmith. Many authors of what Howells would have been happy to acknowledge as "the higher sort of fiction" did indeed earn huge sums of money from their work – Dickens and Zola are two examples – but aside from unanswerable questions of artistic value, there was clearly a real demarcation between wealthy, best-selling writers and their impecunious comrades in literary labor.[25] The division between businessmen and workers has its counterpart, and subdivision, in a division between successful men of letters and hacks or failures.

In relation to the first quotation from the essay (p. 89), the comparison takes on a further dimension. In terms of the two types of writer, it is obvious that one produces for "the most cultivated of the classes," the other for "the masses." With regard to both its producers and its consumers, then, the distinction between art and worthless (but "essential") work is identical to the distinction between the middle or upper and the working classes. Yet only a page later, Howells calmly reaffirms the absolute separation of art from worldly matters:

In so far as the artist is a man of the world, he is the less an artist, and if he fashions himself upon fashion, he deforms his art.[26]

For Howells, the notion of the uniqueness of creative art collapses into cultural élitism, and raises the question of whether all such contemporary theories of art as an absolute value were merely rationalizations (with all that the word implies in "business" terms) of a new state of affairs. Artistic and literary production had unquestionably become part of the general commercial fabric of the nineteenth-century world. The Romantic figure of the artist as genius acquired all the more defensive rhetorical force from the existence of men doing superficially the same kind of work, from whom he must be distinguished.

It is worth remarking that in one sense at least, the unique-ness of the author (whatever his endowments) was a literal fact. In an era before computers or xerox machines, the original manuscript was an irreplaceable item until transposed to the printing press: both Dreiser and Gissing, for instance, were vic-tims of hair-raising incidents when hand-written novels tem-porarily disappeared in transit. By the same token, authors were unlike upholsterers or undertakers in that no two pro-duced an identical product, and some significance surely lies in the fact that the future author of *An American Tragedy* canceled his booking on the doomed *Titanic*.[27] But the artisanal analogy used by Trollope and Howells also draws attention to the fact that authors, working at home and making an individual pro-duct bearing no resemblance to the book or article into which it would eventually be transformed, were a historical anomaly within the workings of an increasingly mechanized industry.

For naturalist authors, the complex position occupied by the artist in contemporary society took on a particular interest which is demonstrated by the fact that Dreiser, Gissing and Zola all wrote novels about the literary and artistic world of their time. While the defenders of realism and naturalism were explicitly opposed to the idealist tendencies of the Romantic view of art, they still tended to seek ways of attributing distinctive if not subversive power to art and artists. Zola's means of accommodating this to his general model was to posit an equally scientific notion of heredity as the biological bearer of personal flaws and talents distinct from those produced by the social milieu. This leads, in *L'Œuvre*, to questions about the compatibility of revolutionary art and public success.

Authors themselves, however, were more interesting to the public, on whose goodwill their livelihoods depended, as unique "personalities," not as social critics or as the representative types which interested them. The question of popular taste and celebrity is one of many artistic and economic dilemmas afflicting the committed, anti-commercial writer in the London of Gissing's *New Grub Street*. Dreiser, on the other hand, had no aesthetic qualms about the involvement of the artist in modern American society. The figure of Eugene Witla in *The "Genius"* has much in common with that of Frank Cowperwood, the business tycoon of the *Trilogy of Desire*, and Witla's moves between art and commerce are strikingly similar to those of his author who, at the time of completing the novel, had just lost a prestigious job as a managing editor for the Butterick Magazines.

The book's equivocal title, however, raises once more the question of individual brilliance in a world impersonally ruled by the economic law of the survival of the fittest. The letter that Dreiser wrote Mencken, explaining his addition of the quotation marks, is fascinating in this respect:

> There is another book, still on sale in old book stores, called *The Genius* – a Russian locale. To avoid being bothered by the author and to convey the exact question which I mean to imply I am quoting my title.[28]

Dreiser claims that there is a real issue specified by the quotes, "the exact question which I mean to imply." But he is led to this refinement only because *The Genius* as a title has lost its originality, having been appropriated by someone else. Authorial uniqueness is nowadays a category regulated by copyrights and professional conventions. Dreiser's compromise of The "Genius" re-establishes legal uniqueness, a legally marketable "Genius," by making genius into an aesthetic question; and that is the order of interest.

The detail is emblematic of the naturalist writers' relation to their artistic work. The nature of art or artistic production is not something that can be considered in isolation, but only with regard to the contemporary commercial order of which it is a part. But the question of "genius" remains, in that context, significant, and makes for some characteristically different viewpoints when the novelists come to look at their own milieu.

7

Making it:
Gissing's
New Grub Street

A famous passage in *New Grub Street* describes a moment's delightful misreading on the part of Marian Yule, fatigued laborer of the literary soils of the British Museum:

> Oh, to go forth and labour with one's hands, to do any poorest, commonest work of which the world has truly need! It was ignoble to sit here and support the paltry pretence of intellectual dignity. A few days ago her startled eye had caught an advertisement in the newspaper, headed "Literary Machine"; had it then been invented at last, some automaton to supply the place of such poor creatures as herself, to turn out books and articles? Alas! the machine was only one for holding volumes conveniently, that the work of literary manufacture might be physically lightened. But surely before long some Edison would make the true automaton; the problem must be comparatively a simple one. Only to throw in a given number of old books, and have them reduced, blended, modernised into a single one for today's consumption.[1]

Several issues which the novel treats in detail are contained in this. Marian sees her work as a writer as an anachronism, something which ought to be done not by "such poor creatures as herself," but by "some automaton" perfectly programed to meet the requirements of present-day industry. In old-fashioned literary language ("Oh, to go forth and labour with one's hands") she dreams of an escape from books, a personal retreat into a pre-industrial culture of the land. But she adds to this the wish that her work be something "of which the world has truly need." Implicitly what she produces now does not have this quality; yet she assumes, like Howells on novels and circuses, a necessity of a different order in the maintenance of the modern system "for today's consumption." It is the solution of a scientific "problem" which would set her free: mechanization is a condition of her liberation from it. So it makes sense that she encounters what she takes as her offer of freedom in the modern, mass-produced context of a newspaper advertisement.

For Marian, who at present is "not a woman, but a mere machine for reading and writing," becoming a woman implies emancipation from "the manufacture of printed stuff which no one ever pretended to be more than a commodity for the day's market" (VIII, 137). Against this perception of alienated labor and "artificial misery" (VIII, 139), however, is the radically different outlook of Jasper Milvain, the type of a successful man of letters in the modern world. If Marian complains of not having the means of being a woman, Jasper considers women as knowable types with potentially predictable behavior: he calls Marian "a good example of the modern literary girl," and declares elsewhere:

> "I have by no means completed my study of women yet. It is one of the things in which I hope to be a specialist some day, though I don't think I shall ever make use of it in novels – rather, perhaps, in life." (V, 97)

The attitude, as with the department store owner, is that of the master. Instead of being himself the machine, Milvain regards other people potentially in that light, as clearly definable objects ("women" as a group or category) which can be rationally analyzed by the potential "specialist" and then utilized for whatever profitable purpose they seem best fitted to serve.[2]

Both Marian and Jasper think of the ruling order as mechanical; the difference between them is that Marian is passively oppressed by it, while Jasper takes it for granted that he is in control and can turn the mechanical world to his own account. Like Marian, he visits the British Museum – not, however, regularly, with Marian's daily shiftwork, but now and then, when he requires the odd piece of information. She laments the pointlessness of production for the commodity market; for Jasper, Marian's category of true "need" or intrinsic worth is not a relevant part of the question:

> "The truth is, I have been collecting ideas, and ideas are convertible into coins of the realm, my boy; I have the special faculty of an extempore writer. Never in my life shall I do anything of solid literary value; I shall always despise the people I write for. But my path will be that of success." (VI, 105)

If Marian regards herself as confined within the "featureless prison limit" (VIII, 148) of the Museum, Jasper, by contrast, is outside walking freely on the "path" of "success." His capacity for "extempore" work puts him beyond the limits of the historic institution where Marian toils away at her pedantic father's dry researches, and rather than feeling himself personally violated by conversion into the status of a machine, he treats his mind and thoughts as resources, as tools distinct from himself. It is his "special faculty" and assembled "ideas" which are "convertible into coins of the realm." Marian harks back to an older

---

Illustration 9   Advertisements around books, King's Cross Station, 1910. Station bookstalls epitomize the trend away from lasting, costly books towards ephemeral, easily affordable volumes available for casual purchase. The cheap, rapid read of the railway novel made the book into an object of immediate consumption, to be devoured and thrown away.

economy and does not mention money at all; for Jasper, it is the medium through which his mental exertions are transformed into the continual end of "success." Whereas Jasper, in his command of the system, frankly admits to a scorn for "the people I write for," Marian does not personalize the readers of commodity literature, seeing them only in the mechanical terms of "today's consumption," an abstract receptacle for the products of a machine in which she is an equally passive working part.

The relatively mechanical and monetary ordering of literature – in its values, its producers, its publication and consumption – is assumed or invoked throughout *New Grub Street*, and always implicitly by way of comparison with a different state of affairs which formerly existed. As Amy Reardon counsels her novel-writing husband: "Art must be practised as a trade, at all events in our time. This is the age of trade" (V, 91). Literature has lost its distinctness as an "art," and become absorbed into the general logic of "trade." The novel itself formally reproduces this dominant rationality of mechanical order in its grouping of characters around pairs of symmetrically opposite terms: old and new, passive and active, idealists and pragmatists. The same counterparts represent thematically the historical trajectory which the narrative, and its characters, assume in the recent or ongoing takeover of art by commerce.[3]

There is a strong historical basis for such polarizations, which is emphasized by the precise setting of the novel's action in the early 1880s. Gissing writes with the hindsight of a decade, during which the forces tending towards the increasingly industrial organization of literature had been further consolidated. The Society of Authors was established in 1884; *Tit-Bits*, the gossipy weekly on which the novel's *Chit-Chat* draws, was started in 1881; and the general scope and scale of the publishing industry was expanding at its fastest-ever rate.[4] Like other consumer-oriented industries developing at the time, such as fashion and tourism, publishers enthusiastically made use of promotional advertising.[5] It is also worth stressing that the end of the

102

nineteenth century was probably the high point of social and economic significance for fictional literature, supplying a vastly increased readership of literate people, and as yet unchallenged by the subsequent arrivals of cinema, radio and television in the field of popular culture.[6]

For the authors of *New Grub Street*, the expansion of the mass market offers a choice between two starkly different alternatives. Just as Marian Yule could only cease to be a machine through increased mechanization, so an exceptional author can only become known – and can only live – by selling his works as commodities. Reardon finds it impossible to compromise his integrity by writing pot-boilers to support his wife and child, and Biffen, who has no dependants, makes a deliberate choice to do without material comforts in order to write the novel he knows has no chance of success in the market. These two die, unable to compromise their resistance; but meanwhile "blessed money" remains the "root of all good, until the world invent some saner economy" (XI, 185). Jasper declares to Marian:

> "If I were rich, I should be a generous and good man; I know I should. So would many another poor fellow whose worst features come out under hardship. This isn't a heroic type; of course not. I am a civilised man, that's all." (VII, 149)

Having money, as for Jedwood, is a means and a prerequisite to the expression of other values. Money is the universal medium, determining not only the particular fate of products bought and sold, but the very roots of character or "type" for those who live within its "featureless limits." As John Goode puts it:

> Realism and adaptability define an area of freedom in a highly determined world – it is crucial to our understanding of the novel that we shouldn't just think of Milvain as an appalling cynic.[7]

Milvain, who manages and manipulates the profession of author with superb facility, serves as a point of contrast with other, less adaptable, comrades or competitors. He aims at success, defined in terms of "money and reputation" (VIII, 149); it is thus a matter of indifference to him that what he produces is, by his own admission, "rubbish" (XIV, 214). Having no pretensions to "genius" – a category which he recognizes and explicitly exempts from his general policy – he adapts his literary product to the changing conditions of marketability. In this, he is up to date both on a month-to-month basis, and in the wider historical perspective by which he differentiates himself from a man like Edwin Reardon:

> "He is the old type of unpractical artist; I am the literary man of 1882. He won't make concessions, or rather, he can't make them; he can't supply the market... I am learning my business. Literature nowadays is a trade. Putting aside men of genius, who may succeed by mere cosmic force, your successful man of letters is your skilful tradesman. He thinks first and foremost of the markets; when one kind of goods begins to go off slackly, he is ready with something new and appetising. He knows perfectly all the possible sources of income. Whatever he has to sell he'll get payment for it... Reardon... sells a manuscript as if he lived in Sam Johnson's Grub Street. But our Grub Street of to-day is quite a different place: it is supplied with telegraphic communication, it knows that literary fare is in demand in every part of the world, its inhabitants are men of business, however seedy." (I, 39)

This vision of an ever-widening range of markets to be exploited by the adept entrepreneur managing his telegraphic empire is the reverse of Marian Yule's conception of the Museum researchers as "hapless flies caught in a huge web" (VIII, 138) – the food itself of "literary fare," rather than its merchants. Milvain's man uses the network instead of being used by it.

Mental skill is one ingredient of Jasper's recipe for success: "We people of brains are justified in supplying the mob with the food it likes" (1, 43). But this is not enough. "It is not merit that succeeds in my line; it is merit *plus* opportunity" (XXXIV, 509). By "opportunity," he means first of all money: independent income, like Whelpdale's, or a small income to get started – and also the "friends" and "influence" which it can provide:

> "Without it, one spends the best part of one's life in toiling for that first foothold which money could at once purchase. To have money is becoming of more and more importance in a literary career; principally because to have money is to have friends. Year by year, such influence grows of more account." (I, 59)

It is at this point that the rationality of the modern machine – though not of Milvain's skills in working it – goes a little awry. Money is necessary as a means to make money and so there is no pure correspondence between merit and reward. And money's accomplice, knowing the right people, is only a new version of patronage. The profession of literary agent came into being during the 1880s (Whelpdale is an example in the novel), and this was a logical rationalization of the system. But personal influence could continue to operate with less explicitly financial kinds of contract. Jasper himself uses the social services of a Mrs Boston Wright who presides at weekly *soirées* and edits a magazine called *The English Girl*. But in the commercial, telegraphic world the personal connection is formulated in thoroughly objective, contemporary terms: "It's a splendid advertisement to have her for a friend" (XII, 194).

Individualism for Jasper extends to the point of his deploring the possibility that old Mr Yule's money may have been left for a municipal park where he lived, rather than to some of the relatives with whom he was never particularly close: "Confound his public purposes!" (XX, 308). Jasper subscribes

---

Illustration 10 Advertisements within books. In an 1892 cheap "yellowback" edition of Gissing's *New Grub Street*, literature and advertising lend support to each other's values. On the left, the new cheap novels parade as "literary fare" for consumption, and on the right the baby food is backed by the cultural cachet of the Bard himself. The photo shown here gave Gissing the idea for his short story, "A Calamity at Tooting."

MELLIN'S FOOD.

MISS BARBER.   Age 15 months.

"4th March, 1889.   96, Brixton Hill, London.
MRS. E. BARBER writes :—"I beg to forward photo. of my little girl, brought up entirely on your Food."

MELLIN'S FOOD BISCUITS.

Palatable, Digestive, Nourishing, Sustaining.   Price 2s. and 3s. 6d. per Tin.
Per post, 2s. 4d. and 4s.

SHAKESPEARIAN WISDOM on the FEEDING and REARING of INFANTS,

A pamphlet of quotations from Shakespeare and portraits of beautiful children, together with testimonials, which are of the highest interest to all mothers.   To be had, with samples, free by post, on application to

G. MELLIN, Marlboro' Works, PECKHAM, LONDON, S.E.

unequivocally to the Social Darwinist philosophy by which fortune favors the fittest to survive: he does not advocate an egalitarian redistribution for the benefit of those who do not succeed in "the rough and tumble of the world's labour-market" (XXXI, 462). Better, then, a select few endowed with "independent" means, than a feeble dissipation giving no-one any power.

The perpetuation of the existing class structure which this implies is part of the explanation for Milvain's meticulous observation of social proprieties. "Civilized" behavior costs nothing and does not engage the sincerity of the "heroic" ideal from which he distinguishes it. It also permits a personal detachment from outward forms of convention and language, like professional objectivity in relation to market strategy: "I am cool-headed enough to make society serve my own ends" (XXII, 333). This is the logic of self-advertisement for individual business purposes, successfully grafted onto an older order of etiquette and hierarchy.

Milvain's lack of concern for questions of intrinsic value leads him, without contradiction, to treat people as well as literature as commodities, to be estimated according to the money or prestige they represent. Advertising himself is part of this, since "modesty helps a man in no department of modern life. People take you at your own valuation" (III, 69). In relation to others, it leads to the switching of affection from one woman to another according to the change in their relative wealth. The novel emphasizes this objectivity by making Marian and Amy interchangeable in another way: as cousins, they share the same name of Yule.

Milvain's valuation of everything in monetary terms extends to his use of time which, like the various markets for books, can be precisely quantified and divided into remunerative segments. He gives this account of a typical working day to his sister Maud:

"I got up at 7.30, and whilst I breakfasted I read through a volume I had to review. By 10.30 the review was written – three-quarters of a column of the *Evening Budget* . . . From 10.30 to 11, I smoked a cigar and reflected, feeling that the day wasn't badly begun. At eleven, I was ready to write my Sunday *causerie* for the *Will o' the Wisp*; it took me till close upon one o'clock, which was rather too long. I can't afford more than an hour and a half for that job. At one, I rushed out to a dirty little eating-house in Hampstead Road. Was back again by a quarter to two, having in the meantime sketched a paper for *The West End.* Pipe in mouth, I sat down to leisurely artistic work; by five, half the paper was done; the other half remains for tomorrow. From five to half-past I read four newspapers and two magazines, and from half-past to a quarter to six I jotted down several ideas that had come to me while reading. At six I was again in the dirty eating-house, satisfying a ferocious hunger. Home once more at 6.45, and for two hours wrote steadily at a long affair I have in hand for *The Current.* Then I came here, thinking hard all the way . . . Have I earned a night's repose?"

"And what's the value of it all?" asked Maud.

"Probably from ten to twelve guineas, if I calculated." (XIV, 213)

Jasper is his own machine, working regular shifts noted with quarter-hour precision, refueled in the "dirty eating-house" to keep itself going, and earning its hours of unproductive "repose" which are the conditions of its repeating the same performance the following day. His economy of daily management succeeds in getting the maximum output from the mind and its supporting physical body, in the knowledge that this will be wholly convertible into the "value" of money (not what his sister meant by the word).

For Milvain, two senses of "making it" are efficiently incorporated or welded together.[8] The poet as earthly maker of immortal verse is not one of them: Milvain makes it in the publishing business and makes the text on which the profit is based. At once capitalist and worker, his objectification of his own mental techniques (the machine), his "ideas" (the raw materials) and his labor (the "hand" that holds the pen) enables him to sit comfortably smoking a cigar in the manager's chair, reflecting on the smooth running of his enterprise.

In Reardon's case, things (and minds) do not work so well:

> The ordering of his day was thus. At nine, after breakfast, he sat
> down to his desk, and worked till one. Then came dinner,
> followed by a walk. As a rule he could not allow Amy to walk
> with him, for he had to think over the remainder of the day's
> toil, and companionship would have been fatal. At about half-
> past three he again seated himself, and wrote until half-past six,
> when he had a meal. Then once more to work from half-past
> seven to ten. Numberless were the experiments he had tried
> for the day's division. The slightest interruption of the order
> for the time being put him out of gear. (IX, 134)

The premises are no different from Milvain's. The writer is a
machine which must not be "put . . . out of gear" and a worker
whose day is ordered into sections of nourishment, exertion
and rest. The two combined can be rationally subjected to
"numberless . . . experiments" for the improvement of productivity. But working against this is a notion of the writer as
human, lacking in "companionship," with a note of despair in
the statement that it would have been "fatal." There is none of
Milvain's suave assurance of the specific periodicals for which
his work is being done, but rather an oppressive extension of
indefinite "toil."

Reardon lives "on the border-land of imbecility" (IX, 153)
because he believes in literary value but has to produce for
monetary value. The contradiction between artist and worker
cum businessman does not exist for Milvain, who is interested
only in the latter terms. For Reardon, it is symbolized by the
two clocks of the church and the workhouse, chiming discor-
dantly outside his window as a reminder of the clash between
cider, stable values and the inhuman mechanisms of modern
times.[9] The clocks also mark the time that Reardon cannot
force into linear regularity in his own daily life: the attempt to
write a novel for the market is a painful matter of "endless cir-
cling, perpetual beginning, followed by frustration" (IX, 153).

This inharmonious pattern of attempted regularity thwarted
by personal incapacity is strikingly similar to what Gissing
records of his own day-to-day life. As with both Reardon and

Milvain, there is a meticulous notation of quantified work and times, as in this typical diary entry from 1894:

> Rain all day. Worked 9.30 to 1, 5 to 8.30, and 9.30 to 10, doing 5 pp.[10]

In the same way, he regards his own life and labors as a machine to be economically used and maintained. Thus it is in terms of the waste of overhead costs that he notes (a week after completing *New Grub Street*!) that he cannot manage the "Walter Scottian work" of early morning writing:

> Find it useless to get up before 10 now-a-days, as I only burn oil and coal to no profit.

Milvain cheerfully begins the day at 7.30, and in other respects also Gissing's practices and preoccupations resemble much more the "mental impotence" of Reardon (XV, 227) than the efficient performance of his friend. He will spend an "evening in fruitless muddling over my story," or a night in "a horrible anguish of clockwork thought about the novel." *New Grub Street* itself was written with just the same wretchedness of endless false starts and fresh beginnings as the experience of Reardon it describes: "No sleep at night. No work to-day. Misery." Like Reardon's "toil," Gissing's is a hellish work of "*fiction-grinding*," interrupted all the time by an all too unmystical writing block:

> Black, black; another hideous day. Not a line of writing. Too horrible to speak of.[11]

Unable to train his mind to the programed exercises of Milvain's "mental gymnastics" (XIV, 214), Reardon longs for a return to the stability of his former position as a wage-earning clerk "with no soul dependent on him" (XI, 180).[12] The "soul" here refers to his wife, but the word also evokes Reardon's inability to do without the "heroic" attitude to life which Milvain regards as anachronistic. Mechanical work and heroic soul are fatally joined in the daily "toil," and the nightly hours permitted for the machine to rest are therefore as much of a trial as those prescribed for working, because of the "morbid conscientiousness" (IV, 79) which inhibits its regular functioning. Thus for Reardon, as for Gissing:

> He seldom slept, in the proper sense of the word; as a rule, he was conscious all through the night of "a kind of fighting" between physical weariness and wakeful toil of the mind . . . The feeling of unmanliness in his own position tortured him into a mood of perversity. (XV, 222-3)

The problem of "unmanliness" here recalls Trollope's upbraiding of the "unmanly" writer claiming the necessarily erratic rhythms of his work. Gissing would no doubt have found a perverse aptness in Trollope's likening of his work to an undertaker's commissions. For Gissing, writing was indeed an existential matter which should not have to be mixed up with the bread and butter of making a living, and it is from this contradiction that the inhibition of production (or creativity) arises.

Milvain's social life is a form of relaxation "earned" by a good day's work. This integration of functions is not available to Reardon in his attempt to become a machine, for whom "companionship would have been fatal" and "the slightest interruption . . . put him out of gear." The same phrase occurs in the diary, when Gissing states, after receiving an unexpected visitor: "Of course it put me out of gear, as every social obligation always does."[13] Yet only three weeks after this, he records of a German friend:

> In afternoon came Plitt who is just back from Rome. By telling me of an Italian girl who lived with him there he made me so wretched in my loneliness that work was impossible.[14]

Both social relations and the lack of them constitute a human hazard which threatens the mechanical occupation of the author, and the impasse is unresolvable. Unlike Milvain, for whom the value of a wife is relative to her financial standing, Reardon craves the exclusiveness of an unchanging and absolute "communion" (V, 96) between two people whose personalities are not determined by social valuations and conditions:

"You know what I *am*. Do you only love the author in me? Don't you think of me apart from all that I may do or not do? If I had to earn my living as a clerk, would that make me a clerk in soul?" (XV, 229)

This tendency to believe in the existence of intrinsic values for literature and people is Reardon's fatal flaw (in his terms) or maladjustment (in a "practical" man's). And since rational, practical behavior is associated with modern life, it makes sense that its antithesis, for Reardon and for Gissing, should take the form of an idealization of a historically distant past, that of Ancient Greece. The value of Greece is always stated by means of an implicit comparison with the present. So on Homer: "*That* was not written at so many pages a day, with a workhouse clock clanging its admonition at the poet's ear" (IX, 155). Reardon and his friend Biffen are passionately attached to the Greek verse which is dissociated for them from the workaday rhythms of economic necessity:

> For half an hour the two men talked Greek metres as if they lived in a world where the only hunger known could be satisfied by grand or sweet cadences. (X, 172)

There is never any suggestion that the ideal is something which might be capable of realization in the modern world. Instead, it functions as a kind of private dream protecting the man against the harshness of objective reality, as when Reardon roams the streets of London muttering "some example of sweet or sonorous metre which had a soothing effect upon him" (XXV, 376). Although the "gaunt wildness" of his appearance might indicate the subversive figure of the Romantic artist, in the modern city he simply looks "disreputable . . . to passers-by":[15]

> These seedy habiliments were the tokens of his degradation, and at times he regarded them (happening to see himself in a shop mirror) with pleasurable contempt. (XXV, 377)

Reardon, like Milvain, knows himself to be no "genius" but only a "mediocrity" (IV, 83), and he is no more interested than the latter in changing the conditions of the world he lives in. But instead of assimilating them to his own advantage like Milvain, Reardon adopts a position of arrogant spectatorship. Confronted by the evidence of modern commercialism, he returns the store's reflection of his artistic "degradation" with a look as powerless as it is disdainful.

The classical ideal does take on a kind of reality for Reardon when he goes on an actual visit to Greece. But it is only a temporary respite, the tourist's limited escape from everyday experience. The twenty pounds he urges Biffen to "scrape together" for the same purpose (XXVII, 406) is the way to an attainment necessarily fleeting and salvaged from memory of that "ideal world . . . which seems to me, when I recall it, bathed in diviner light" (XXVII, 407). And there is also the risk that today's Mediterranean may not live up to expectations, as when Gissing records his own "mood of anger with modern Italians, who ruin all the old associations."[16]

The solipsism of the artistic dream is nicely conveyed by a letter the author wrote to his brother Algernon, following a visit to the Academy where he saw

> bright sea pictures, with their marvellous reproductions of sun, shade, foam and translucent water. In fact, I can't really say whether I don't derive more positive pleasure from a fine picture of such things than from the reality. In many ways there is a grievous discomfort attending on a ramble among fine scenery – weariness of limb, heat of sun, showers, dust, wind. Whereas, in looking at a picture your imagination enables you to realize at the full every agreeable sensation, without any of the discomforts. To be sure, it also makes you wish for the time to be in face of the reality, but it is a shallow philosophy which makes much of this.[17]

"Positive pleasure" is assured by the contemplation of art, and the "discomfort" of physical uncertainties in "the reality" could only detract from this. So Greece remains an "ideal world," valued the more for its comforting distance from the

114

conditions of "the human sphere," as little subject to modification as "sun, showers, dust, wind."

Bygone ideals of literature and life have force as references for both progressive and passive inhabitants of New Grub Street, and there is both irony and realism when Whelpdale, by now one of the adaptable survivors among modern men of letters, tells the story of his experiences as a starving author living on peanuts in Troy, NY.[18] But whereas a Milvain will contrast "heroic" with "civilized" or "the man of business" with the "dreamy literary fellow" (XXXIII, 503) to stress his own modernity, a Reardon helplessly asserts the higher reality of values expressible only in terms of their difference from those of contemporary life. Thus artistic ideals necessarily take on a social meaning different from any they may have had in classical Greece or Shakespeare's England, if only because it derives from their opposition to particular modern forms of life which were not in existence then. This, in ideological terms, is the structural polarity experienced by working idealistic writers as an absolute contradiction between the two incompatible extremes of the art and the trade, the poet and the machine.

Alfred Yule, the "battered man of letters" (II, 48), who represents in effect a dead or dysfunctional combination of both the literary and the professional, is an interesting variant. Although, as with Milvain, "ambition devoured him," it is a century out of date in its direction: "Practically he was living in a past age; his literary ideals were formed on the study of Boswell" (VII, 127). The eighteenth-century Grub Street is never a focus of nostalgia in Gissing's novel, and Yule's classicism has the futile aridity of a Casaubon's, lacking in the restorative solace of the metrical camaraderie of Reardon and Biffen. Yule's own circle of cronies is in fact presented as a *Dunciad* of tedious, competitive backbiters. And this is the style in which his senile hopes of editing a learned periodical are mocked: "The joy of sitting in that dictatorial chair! The delight of having his own organ once more . . . !" (VII, 127).

115

The fantasy, like Yule's tyrannical treatment of his daughter, is thus represented as a grotesque abuse of true literary values.

It is as if any rapprochement between ideal and pragmatic, artistic and professional values must be doomed or treated as obsolete. Biffen is the only author who expresses a form of social commitment, but his "mission of literary realism" (XXXV, 529) in writing *Mr Bailey, Grocer* is not expected to appeal to the class it singles out as worthy of literary portrayal: "The working classes detest anything that tries to represent their daily life" (XXVIII, 416). In the novel's scheme, the choice is simply between the production of trite popular magazines for (but not by) "the quarter-educated" (XXXIII, 496) and the creation of serious art for a select few. On an individual level there can, perhaps, be some communication, as with the working man to whom Biffen teaches "comperstition" (XVI, 242). But this is only to emphasize the personal nature of art, clinging to a "sincerity" of its own which is contrasted with an assumed amorality or immorality in production for a large audience.[19]

The élitist attitude which this suggests is evident throughout Gissing's writings; the following passage is from an essay of 1895 called "Why I don't write plays":

> Our thronging multitude, with leisure and money undreamt of by their predecessors, must somehow find amusement after a day-time of more or less exhausting labour; to supply the amusement is naturally a profitable business; and so it comes about that the literary ideal of a stage-play is supplanted on the stage itself by the very practical notions of a popular impresario. Hence the sundering of theatre and literature . . . . At present we can be grateful that one form of literary art . . . can be cultivated regardless of the basest opinion. Professed playwrights may be left to entertain their admirers. A novelist who would deliberately contend with them has to study a craft which goes, or ought to go, sorely against his conscience.[20]

The total "sundering" here of popular theatre and "the literary ideal" rests on the premise that the leisure now available to the working classes can only be occupied by something that is artistically worthless, both because it is "amusement" and because it is "a profitable business." The very necessity of popular art ("must somehow find amusement") implicates it in "practical notions" incompatible with the "ideal." The triviality ascribed to playwrights, who "may be left to entertain their admirers," is not contested as their right; on the contrary, it is an inevitable state of affairs from which the novelist can only withdraw into the private integrity of "his conscience."

Far from living on peanuts, Jasper Milvain gets himself on the road to success by writing material whose value is "equal to that of the contents of a mouldy nut" (XIV, 214). "Rubbish" sells, while sorely labored literature is treated as trash. Thus Biffen ruefully acknowledges the absurdity of his work from a modern point of view when he risks his life to save the manuscript of *Mr Bailey* and then speculates on what might have happened if he had failed:

> The *Daily Telegraph* would have made a leader out of me. "This poor man was so strangely deluded as to the value of a novel in manuscript which it appears he had just completed, that he positively sacrificed his life in the endeavour to rescue it from the flames." And the *Saturday* would have had a column of sneering jocosity on the irrepressibly sanguine temperament of authors. At all events, I should have had my day of fame. (XXXI, 473)

Fame for a day, or not at all; personality or sincerity; popularity or withdrawal; prestige or eccentricity: these are the divisions connoted by the split between artist and machine in the dualistic world of *New Grub Street*. There is nothing outside the rigid dichotomies of value and class entailed by the starting assumption that culture is incompatible with the new commerce and the mass society it caters to: no way out of the impasse which offers an impossible choice between "practical" adaptation to profit-seeking vulgarity, and the noble resistance of starving, embittered authenticity.

8

The artist as adman:
Dreiser's
The "Genius"

The "Genius" is 736 pages long, a fact noted with less than laudatory emphasis by many of its reviewers when the book first appeared in 1915. Quantity, with authors "paid by the word," might seem to be a virtue in Howells' parodic scheme of modern literary productivity, but it is in these terms that the objection is made, and this for a book which had already been cut by something like a third of its original length. It was not a critical success any more than a popular one, and such sales as it did have were inflated by the notoriety that followed from suppression through the influence of a society for moral reform,[1] and subsequent republication a decade later. In academic criticism over the years, *The "Genius"* has received very little attention apart from that of biographical critics interested in the many parallels between Dreiser's life and that of the book's painter hero, Eugene Witla.[2] Larzer Ziff summarizes the situation when he says that "the only literary figure who ever rated *The "Genius"* as first among the novels of Theodore Dreiser was Theodor Dreiser"; and he adds, laconically, "His reasons were personal rather than literary."[3]

Yet there was an element in the contemporary journalistic criticism which saw in the book qualities of social rather than

118

individual inclusiveness. Writing in the New York *Herald*, James L. Ford objects to the form of the book on the grounds that

> Story telling is something more than a mere recital of facts and incidents. But as a hundred reel film of everything that might actually happen to a young man during the early years of his life *The "Genius"* leaves nothing to be desired.[4]

This is not offered as praise; John Cowper Powys, however, is ready to hail a new Homer on the same grounds:

> It is the Prose-Iliad of the American scene . . . Dreiser is the true master of the American Prose-Epic just because he is not afraid of the weariness, the staleness, the flatness and unprofitableness of actual human conversation.[5]

Both writers base their case not on the novel's idiosyncratic or autobiographical qualities, but on its supposed representativeness as an impersonal transcript of modern American life.

The difference between the personal and the general can easily slide into a contrast between the distinctive and the banal. Ford's derogatory allusion to the new popular entertainment of the early twentieth century suggests a further extension of the dichotomy into social terms. This becomes explicit in *Vogue*'s review:

> He employs habitually . . . the cant of any trade with which he is dealing. He thinks "individual" a synonym for "man;" such phrases as these are frequent: "salable art feature," "society man," "as low as could possibly be figured," "Eugene 'stated' to Colfax," "exclusive restaurant," "he must behave himself," "a record price." Several of the characters talk like muckers; not one has the speech of a gentleman. Mr Dreiser seems to have acquired about all that a brilliant man can acquire except taste.[6]

The berated examples of contemporary idioms, involving particular ways of referring to money or social status, are condemned as incompatible with something identified as the "taste" of a "gentleman": the author's lack of this quality is inseparable from his indiscriminate employment of the jargon of modern American "trade." The style and form of *The "Genius"* reinforce the question implied by the equivocal title: the nature and social place of "art" in the world of the "salable art feature" and nickelodeon.

The *Vogue* critic fails to mention that there is in fact a proper gentleman to be found in the novel's pages, and his role says much about the assumed historical schema in the progression of art. Eugene Witla, the artist-hero, is working as a magazine illustrator in New York when opportunity comes in the form of one M. Anatole Charles, manager of a prestigious firm of art dealers:

> M. Anatole Charles spoke English almost more than perfectly. He was . . . polished, dignified, immaculately dressed, conservative in thought and of few words in expression . . . . He was most anxious to find talent – profitable talent – though on occasion . . . the house of Kellner and Son was not averse to doing what it could for art – and that for art's sake without any thought of profit whatsoever.[7]

But this old-world European manner of putting "art" before profit is not part of Eugene's own estimate of the value of his work:

> Did the world wish this sort of thing? Would it ever buy of him? Was he of any real value? (II, V, 216)

Eugene's concern is at all times with "building up a paying reputation" (I, **XX**, 131), with value recognized in salability. There is thus no contradiction for him between painting pictures and earning $25,000 a year as advertising manager of a large corporation, any more than there was for the author of *Sister Carrie* in becoming an editor at Butterick's. Both are simply ways of making a living and a name:

> "My dear lady," Eugene once said solemnly, "I can't live by

painting pictures as I am living by directing magazines. Art is
very lovely. I am satisfied to believe that I am a great painter.
Nevertheless, I made little out of it, and since then I have
learned to live. It's sad, but it's true. If I could see my way to
live in half the comfort I am living in now and not run the risk
of plodding the streets with a picture under my arm, I would
gladly return to art." (II, III, 502)

Economic considerations are primary, and art is a luxury which
takes second place in the order of time and value. It makes
sense, then, that the high point of Eugene's working life is
epitomized by his sumptuous office at the top of the new
eighteen-story building of the United Magazines Corporation,
his occupation of which occurs at the same time that he and his
wife Angela move into an apartment on Riverside Drive, "the
apex of social glory" (II, XLI, 458).

Yet if it seems that the values and aims of the man of art are
identical with those of the man of business, the text sometimes
implies otherwise. When their joint employer introduces Witla
to White, his designated rival at United, two different types
confront each other:

> Eugene saw White as an interesting type – tall, leathery,
> swaggering, a back-street bully evolved into the semblance of a
> gentleman. White saw in Eugene a nervous, refined, semi-
> emotional literary and artistic type who had, however, a
> curious versatility and virility not common among those whom
> he had previously encountered. (II, XL, 454)

Later, White concludes that Eugene is "too artistic, to be really
stable and dependable" (II, XL, 457). There is a rudimentary
aggressiveness in the "bully evolved into the semblance of a
gentleman," which is contrasted to a kind of effete refinement
in the "semi-emotional" artist. This is accentuated by a suggestion of effeminacy in the erratic artistic type, usually without
"virility" or the drive to carry a project through. The aura of
poetic sensibility which surrounds Dreiser's mother in Dawn,
the autobiography on which he was working at the same time as

121

on part of *The "Genius"*,[8] is similar to this; and *A Traveler at Forty*, another autobiographical production of this period, expands the association of the artistic and the feminine:

> I have always thought . . . that the stage is almost the only ideal outlet for the artistic temperament of a talented and beautiful woman . . . . In the main the men of the stage are frail shadows of a much more real thing – the active, constructive man in other lines.[9]

While women are "peculiarly suited to this realm of show, color and make-believe,"[10] for men there is necessarily a conflict between "the artistic temperament" and the "active, constructive" form which their manliness is expected to take.

But there is a further dimension to the question, in that the male artistic temperament also gives rise to an attraction for the feminine as an aesthetic ideal. Early in the story, Eugene breaks off with Ruby Kenny, the working-class girl he has been having an affair with in Chicago; and the narrator comments:

> Had he been soundly introspective, he would have seen that he was an idealist by temperament, in love with the aesthetic, in love with love, and that there was no permanent faith in him for anybody – except the impossible she. (I, XV, 100)

Witla's "idea of the perfection of eighteen," made flesh in a succession of attractive maidens, is in practical life "his undoing" (III, XXVI, 680), and leads eventually to the loss of his job with United Magazines, just as Dreiser fell from grace at Butterick's owing to his involvement with one Thelma Cudlipp. In this connection, the peculiarities of the "idealist" work against him in the eyes of society by attributing to him not a lack of virility but too much: "varietism" is another symptom of instability.

Witla's art, like Dreiser's novels, is realist: contemporary, urban and American. M. Charles responds dramatically to a painting of Eugene's:

> Raw reds, raw greens, dirty grey paving stones – such faces!

Why, this thing fairly shouted its facts. It seemed to say: "I'm dirty, I am commonplace, I am grim, I am shabby, but I am life." And there was no apologizing for anything in it, no glossing anything over. Bang! Smash! Crack! came the facts one after another, with a bitter, brutal insistence on their so-ness. Why, on moody days when he had felt sour and depressed he had seen somewhere a street that looked like this, and there it was – dirty, sad, slovenly, immoral, drunken – anything, everything, but here it was. "Thank God for a realist," he said to himself as he looked. (II, VI, 222-3)

Realism represents the "raw" solidity of "grey paving stones," proudly shouting its "facts" of the filthy street like White, the "leathery, swaggering . . . back-street bully." This is far from the softness of a "refined, semi-emotional literary and artistic type." It appears, then, that what modern realist art can offer is a specifically masculine form of artistic preference which avoids the weakness of feminine sentimentality. This becomes clear through the distinction made between Eugene's and Angela's taste:

In literature, only realism appealed to him; for her, sentiment, strained though not necessarily unreal, had the greatest charm. Art in its purely aesthetic forms meant nothing at all to her. To Eugene it was the last word in the matter of emotional perception. History, philosophy, logic, psychology, were sealed books to her. (I, VIII, 62)[11]

Modern art is thus opposed to weak sentimentalism as a valid outlet for "the active, constructive man"; in fact Dreiser's friend H. L. Mencken, reviewing *The "Genius"*, goes so far as to identify the "artist" side of Eugene with masculine achievement in general. He speaks of

two Witlas – the artist who is trying to create something . . . and the sentimentalist whose longing is to be loved, coddled, kept at ease. This conflict, of course, is at the bottom of the misery of all men above the grade of car conductor, barber, waiter or Sunday school superintendent. On the one hand there is the desire to exert power, to do something that has not

123

been done before, to bend reluctant material to one's will, and on the other hand there is the desire for comfort, for well-being, for an easy life. This latter desire . . . is visualized by women. Women are the conservative and conservators, the enemies of hazard and innovation, the compromizers and temporizers. That very capacity for mothering which is their supreme gift is the greatest of all foes to masculine enterprise. Most men, alas, yield to it. In the common phrase, they marry and settle down.[12]

As much as it makes the artist into an exemplary figure of male achievement, this passage also suggests that the attempt to "create something" through "innovation" is characteristic of the progressive man in general.

If artist and entrepreneur are the same, then Mencken's exclusion from his generalization of the "car conductor, barber, waiter or Sunday school superintendent" makes perfect sense. Creative activity is not open to the lower classes; and yet it is working-class life – cities, factories, street scenes – which the modern artist takes as his subject matter. This, for instance, is how his future career appears to Witla from the window when he takes the train from Chicago to try his luck in the art world of New York:

> He saw men working, and sleeping towns succeeding one another. What a great country America was! What a great thing to be an artist here! Millions of people and no vast artistic voice to portray these things – these simple dramatic things like the coke ovens in the night. If he could only do it! If he could only stir the whole country, so that his name would be like that of Doré in France or Verestchagin in Russia. (I, XIV, 96)

There is no sense here of social mission, but rather of the expansive opportunities offered by America as a means to personal fame.

The artist's prospecting seems in one way to resemble the customary exploitation of "millions of people" for the individualist ends of capitalism. Long before his flirtation with

124

communism in the thirties, Dreiser's view of the order of things at this time is well represented by his response to the industrial area around Manchester, during his stay in England as guest of the genteel publisher Grant Richards:

> I have always marveled at the inequalities of nature – the way it will give one man a low brow and a narrow mind . . . and make a slave or horse of him, and another a light, nimble mind, a quick wit and . . . make a gentleman of him . . . I did not make my mind. I did not make my art. I cannot choose my taste except by predestined instinct, and yet here I am sitting in a comfortable English home, as I write, commiserating the poor working man . . . I see in the whole thing no scheme but an accidental one . . . .
>
> But these queer, weird, hard, sad, drab manufacturing cities – what great writer has yet sung the song of them?[13]

The difference between the writer (or businessman) and the worker is purely "accidental," but it is none the less a real one, based on "inequalities of nature" in mental capacity which justify their respective places in the world.

It follows, then, that the artist's natural endowments will raise him to his rightful level in the world, separate from the slaves and horses of a lower order. When Witla, one-time laundry delivery boy in Chicago, goes back to manual work for a spell, it is for personal reasons: as a form of therapy following a mental breakdown. "So radical a thing as day labor for his nerves" (II, XIX, 304) is not intended to bridge the inherent distance between the artist and his fellow workers. To these he "felt superior" (II, XXI, 314), and they could be "heavy clods of souls" who "to his artistic eye, appeared machines, more mechanical than humanly self-directive" (II, XX, 307). It is appropriate, then, that during this experience which gives him "insight into the workaday world" (II, XXI, 313), Eugene is spending his off-duty hours living in a comfortable middle-class home complete with an affluent, intellectual daughter who becomes his mistress. As when Dreiser himself reflects on the mysterious beauties of heavy industry in Britain from his seat on the passing train, Witla remains in the position of a privileged outsider looking on:

> He could sleep and work as a day laborer and take life easy for a while. He could get well now and this was the way to do it. Day laborer! How fine, how original, how interesting. He felt somewhat like a knight-errant reconnoitring a new and very strange world. (II, XIX, 305)

Yet there is a second side to Eugene at this time, expressed through his disagreements with the glamorous Carlotta. While the men at the railroad carpentry shop "lived on another plane, apparently,"

> at the other end of the stream awaiting him was Carlotta, graceful, sophisticated . . . lukewarm in her interest in morals . . . representing in a way a world which lived upon the fruits of this exploited toil and caring nothing about it. If he said anything to Carlotta about the condition of Joseph Mews, who carried bundles of wood home to his sister of an evening to help save the expense of fuel, she merely smiled. If he talked of the poverty of the masses she said, "Don't be doleful, Eugene." She wanted to talk of art and luxury and love. (II, XXIII, 334)

Here Eugene is suggesting a closer concern for social injustice which distances him from his wealthy friend rather than from his working colleagues. The association implied between the last three terms is crucial here, and is reinforced in the previous paragraph by descriptions of three of Eugene's co-workers as lacking in love and art, as well as in luxury: one of them "had only the vaguest conception of the beauty of nature"; another was "scarcely more artistic than the raw piles of lumber with which he dealt"; a third "had no knowledge of the rich emotions of love or of beauty which troubled Eugene's brain" (II, XXIII, 334). Art is a refinement unknown and unappreciable to men who have to carry wood home to save money.

The question is not, however, pursued in social terms. Rather, its very existence as an issue is represented as a result of

Eugene's maladjusted state of mind, sublimely restored when

> there came over him that other phase of his duality – the ability to turn his terrible searchlight of intelligence which swept the heavens and the deep as with a great white ray – upon the other side of the question. It revealed constantly the inexplicable subtleties and seeming injustices of nature. He could not help seeing how the big fish fed upon the little ones, the strong were constantly using the weak as pawns.... The honest man might be very fine but he wasn't very successful. There was a great to-do about morals, but most people were immoral or unmoral. Why worry? Look to your health! Don't let a morbid conscience get the better of you.... The survival of the fittest was the best. Why should he worry? He had talent. (II, XXV, 348)

Since this passage in fact occurs in the context of a debate about the "morality" of Eugene and Carlotta's adulterous relationship, there is a fascinating assimilation going on in it between social conscience and Witla's "peculiar vice" (II, XXV, 347), his addictive love of women. Eugene's breakdown was attributed to sexual over-indulgence, at a time when "he had no knowledge of the effect of one's sexual life upon one's work," its potential damage to "a perfect art" and distortion of "a normal interpretation of life" (II, VIII, 238). Carlotta's attractions, then, threaten a further disintegration of the sanity which consists in self-fulfillment as one of the strong and talented, possessed of a "normal" Social Darwinian indifference to the smaller fish in the sea.

> The licentious were worn threadbare and disgraced by their ridiculous and psychologically diseased propensities. Women and men who indulged in these unbridled relations were sickly sentimentalists, as a rule, and were thrown out or ignored by all forceful society. One had to be strong, eager, determined and abstemious if wealth was to come, and then it had to be held by the same qualities. One could not relax. Otherwise one became much what he was now, a brooding sentimentalist – diseased in mind and body. (II, XXX, 379)

127

Thus is the "sentimentalist" side of the artist dismissed as a sexual aberration, functionally equivalent to the "morbid conscience" against which the virile realist must manifest the strength required "if wealth was to come." The only sane attitude is one of resignation and passivity in regard to social questions, but active commitment to personal survival in a competitive world: "Why worry? Look to your health!"

That the measure of masculine achievement is material gain, in all fields including the artist's, is shown by the subsequent career of Witla, whose cure is marked by his securing the first of the series of jobs on the management side of commercial art and advertising which will ultimately lead him to the top of the United Magazines organization. When Eugene falls once again from a position of power, losing his high-paying job, the immediate reason is the return of the "peculiar vice" in his pursuit of Suzanne Dale; but this is fatally linked to a wish to return to the purely artistic life. "You have changed me so completely," he declares to Suzanne,

> "made me over into the artist again. From now on I can paint again. I can paint you." . . . He felt as though he was revealing himself to himself in an apocalyptic vision. (III, VI, 526)

> He was literally crazed by her . . . . He thought that his art was a gift, that he had in a way been sent to revolutionize art in America . . . . The fates lied. Lovely, blandishing lures were held out only to lead men to destruction. (III, XI, 563)

There is a shade of the virago figure in the "lovely, blandishing lures" of the immaculate painted lady, but here her vengeance is wreaked not so much by destroying the man's art as by restoring it, at the expense of his commercial force. The relationship with Suzanne is explicitly characterized in terms of its distinction from the real world. Eugene "was walking in some elysian realm which had nothing to do with the tawdry evidence of life about him" (III, VII, 530) and expresses the timeless poetry of the experience by quoting lines from Keats' "Ode on a Grecian

128

Urn" (III, VII, 531). When he writes a humble letter to his "Flower Face" during the crisis which follows his dismissal, he declares: "I am not sorry. I have been dreaming a wonderfully sweet and perfect dream" (III, XXII, 650).

If the "dream" is a desirable transcendence of the "tawdry evidence" of the quotidian, there is another sense in which it appears less beneficial. At the end of the same epistolary plea, Eugene writes:

> "I wonder if I have been dreaming a dream. You are so beautiful. You have been such an inspiration to me. Has this been a lure – a will-o'-the-wisp?" (III, XXII, 651)

In this case the dream, far from being a higher, poetic form of truth, is a dangerous distraction that leads away from established paths of progress. In Eugene's letter the contradiction is not acknowledged, while for Suzanne, there is no contradiction, but one harmonious conception which links the two sides of her lover's aspirations:

> Once when they were out in an automobile together, he had asked her why she loved him, and she said, "because you are a genius and can do anything you please."
> "Oh no," he answered, "nothing like that. I can't really do very much of anything. You just have an exaggerated notion of me."
> "Oh, no, I haven't," she replied. "You can paint, and you can write" – she was judging by some of the booklets about Blue Sea and verses about herself and clippings of articles done in his old Chicago newspaper days, which he showed her once in a scrapbook in his apartment – "and you can run that office, and you were an advertising manager and an art director . . .
> "And you love me so beautifully," she added by way of climax. (III, XXII, 652)

This impressive list of genial qualifications, crowned by that of beautiful loving, runs the gamut of Eugene's artistic and commercial achievements, and makes no distinction between them. The "genius" appears in whatever form his activities happen to take.

Part of Suzanne's evidence for Eugene's writing ability comes from her reading of "some of the booklets about Blue Sea," and the detail is significant. This was a land development speculation in which he had invested a great deal of money: a tourist paradise designed to "carry him into the millionaire class" (III, III, 501), and provide "such a dream of beauty and luxury as would turn the vast tide of luxury-loving idlers and successful money grubbers from the former resorts to this" (III, II, 496). It is perfect for Eugene's manifold talents, because "nothing interested him quite so much as beauty and luxury in some artistic combination" (III, II, 496-7): a material realization of the dream that is set apart from the workaday world. Poetic beauty ceases to be an unrealistic "will-o'-the-wisp" in the form of a leisure industry. Everyday life goes hand in hand with a constructed and equally commercialized realm of "art and luxury and love," and Suzanne hits the nub of the question when she innocuously suggests: "I'll be your week-end bride" (III, XII, 579).

The transformation of art into a modern cultural enterprise is clarified by Dreiser in his comments in *A Traveler at Forty* on the irrelevance of old English churches. Having attended a disappointingly dull Christmas service in a country village, he writes:

> Beautiful in its way? Yes. Quaint? Yes. But smacking more of poverty and an ordered system continued past its day than anything else. I felt a little sorry for the old church and the thin rector and the goodly citizens, albeit a little provincial, who clung so

---

Illustration 11   Bon Marché appointments diary, 1915. The Bon Marché calendar is superimposed on the seasons of nature. Not only is the presence of the store made to seem part of nature, but both become tourist attractions for the city-dwellers. Here the attraction of the sale is seen to be stronger than that of the landscape. Also, the poster which slows down the cars is presented as socially useful, doing the work of the country bumpkin's small, illiterate notice: "They all slow down! . . . No more need to put my poster up, then!".

UNE AFFICHE A DEUX FINS

MONSIEUR LE MAIRE. — Ils ralentissent tous !... Plus besoin de mettre mon affiche, alors !...

fatuously to a time-worn form. They have their place, no doubt, and it makes that sweet, old lavender atmosphere which seems to hover over so much that one encounters in England. Nevertheless life does move on . . . . Why not set these old churches aside as museums or art galleries or for any other public use . . .? Let the people tax themselves for things they really do want, skating-rinks, perhaps, and moving pictures.[14]

There is a reference to Herbert Spencer here in the identification of an anachronistic institution and the conviction of a gradual betterment of the human condition; but the specifying of the latter's form in terms of modern leisure industries is a typical Dreiser touch. In a sense, the passage resumes all the phases of Witla's career. The outdated "sweet old lavender atmosphere" of England is like the pastoral associations of his wife's native Wisconsin, which confirm a commitment to her he later feels to have been mistaken.[15] The museums and art galleries recall M. Charles' old-world dedication to art "for art's sake," which aids the young painter's career for a time. But these are irrelevant compared to the skating rinks and moving pictures which, despite the fact that the English admittedly "cling" to their own traditions, the dynamic American advertising director of Eugene's later years can establish as being "things they really want."

The connection between the materialistic evolution of society and of Witla is explicit in the novel:

It seemed to him as though all his life he had naturally belonged to this perfect world of which country houses, city mansions, city and country clubs, expensive hotels and inns, cars, resorts, beautiful women, affected manners, subtlety of appreciation and perfection of appointment generally were the inherent concomitants. This was the true heaven – that material and spiritual perfection on earth, of which the world was dreaming and to which, out of toil, disorder, shabby ideas, mixed opinions, non-understanding and all the ill to which the flesh is heir, it was constantly aspiring. (II, XLIII, 472)

Perhaps, after all, The "Genius" is a true American epic, the upward drift of the artist's career pointing out the way for the general tendency towards "material and spiritual perfection on earth." How appropriate, then, that Mencken's review should evoke a pioneer journey alleviated by a brand-name product when he remarks, "quite academically," that

> a greater regard for fairness of phrase and epithet would be as a flow of Pilsner to the weary reader in his journey across the vast deserts, steppes and pampas of the Dreiserian fable.[16]

9

Working: Zola's
L'Œuvre

The *œuvre* of *L'Œuvre* is the completed work of the artist Claude Lantier: the novel stands as the symbolic masterpiece its hero fails for years to achieve, and as "l'œuvre manqué de sa vie"[1] narratively represented in both its promise and its end. Lantier's painting should have made him

> the necessary man of genius, the one who would embody the formula in masterpieces. What a position to occupy! to tame the mob, to open a century, to create an art! (VII, 254) [2]

As a novel, *L'Œuvre* is about the unfinished business of naturalism as a literary and artistic program; and the double implications of this theme are suggested by one of the many titles Zola considered for the work: *Fin de Siècle*. Radical break or impotent defeat, ongoing project or possible failure: the hesitations are basic to the work, to its questioning of the conditions of modern artistic working and works. Zola summarizes his dual conception in the preliminary outline:

> Then pessimism; but still faith, ultimately a deification of the generative act. And the contradictions, the beginning of an evolution, a start to the 20th century: thence, the useless efforts, the struggles of Claude.[3]

The difference evoked here between historical limits, "l'évolution," and individual achievement, is crucial not only to the fictional fortunes of Claude and his friends, and to the various destinies outside the novel of Zola's naturalist associates on which they are based, but to the entire project of naturalism from the time of its formulation in *Le Roman expérimental*. The program which advocated on the one hand a scientific objectivity on the part of the artist, and on the other a democratic openness of subject matter and licence to practice, automatically undermined the notion of the artist as Romantic genius, against which it was expressly posited. Yet the theory of heredity, which Zola used in tandem with his general evolutionary determinism, allowed for the possibility of individual differences. Thus *tempérament* came to function as a kind of *deus ex machina*, preserving a category of originality or deviation from the norm. Zola says of Lantier when he is planning the character in the *ébauche*: "Naturally I'll make him a naturalist, but he ought to be taken with his personality."[4] In the essay "Du Roman," he goes so far as to defend other members of the Médan literary group from anti-naturalist attacks precisely on the grounds of their originality:

> The truth is that the small number of young realists that some people believe they are squashing under the common epithet of naturalist have quite the most divergent temperaments one could possibly see, not one of them offers the same personality, not one of them looks at humanity from the same angle.[5]

Such a distinction of individuals and perspectives is hardly the form of justification to be expected for the art which Zola describes elsewhere by its generality and community of aim, and its neutrality of style and subject matter.

L'Œuvre, the naturalist novel about art, no less than the theoretical program, is about a group of distinct personalities who, moreover, have much in common with the leading figures in the art world of Zola's time. Certainly, it would have been difficult to write an objective account of this milieu without resorting to personal as opposed to general traits, art being the domain *par excellence* in which great names, the individuals who stand apart from the crowd, are inseparable from the wider trends which they come to represent. Zola's technique, in fact, was to analyze actual artists according to significant traits, which could be reshuffled and recombined to produce the various characters of the novel. In the *ébauche*, he speaks of "l'Alexis," "le Gervex," "un Baille," "une sorte de Valabrègue"; Bongrand will be "un Manet très chic, – un Flaubert plutôt," Claude "Un Manet, un Cézanne dramatisé; plus près de Cézanne" (*Ébauche*, fols. 290, 271, 271, 289, 264).

Exploring the relationship between Zola's characters and the artists he knew in real life, as many have done, is therefore an enterprise sanctioned not only by the individualist nature of the field itself, but also by the writer's own conception of his undertaking. But the interesting questions do not lie in a search for the one-to-one correspondences of a *roman-à-clef* – a proceeding against which the doubleness of some of Zola's allocations quoted above is already warning enough. What matters is not whether Claude is 60 per cent Cézanne and 40 per cent Manet or vice versa, but rather, what Zola took to be the significant traits of the artists of his time, viewed from his particular "angle." Those he saw as characteristic of Gervex converted the individual into a type, "le Gervex," with a particular

---

Illustration 12   The department store in Paris, photographed by Zola from the window of an apartment opposite. With the man positioned as unseen observer of the woman's sphere, the picture focuses the conflation of photographic objectivity and voyeuristic interest in the naturalists' perspective on their subjects. It is near to a form of illicit access, here strongly evoked by the fact that the apartment is that of Jeanne Rozerot, the author's mistress. The proximity of her place to the store further suggests the transgressive overtones of shopping for the bourgeois wife, leaving the marital home to indulge her fantasies elsewhere.

role in the structure of the novel. The same can be said as for personal traits with regard to recognizable, autobiographical incidents which are scattered throughout the novel: the Provençal youth of Zola and Cézanne; the humiliation of Manet at the Salon des Refusés of 1863; the meetings of Zola and his artist friends at the Café Guerbois; the regular Thursday evening suppers of the literary group at Zola's house in the village of Médan. The importance of such elements is not their historical authenticity, but the way that Zola interprets that history when he writes *L'Œuvre* in 1885.[6]

There are many indications that the early 1880s were for Zola a time of transition if not crisis. With the successive deaths of Flaubert (1880), Wagner (1882) and Manet (1883), it seemed, as Patrick Brady writes, that an era had come to an end.[7] The unprecedented sales of *L'Assommoir* and *Nana*[8] had established Zola beyond question as a *maître* and the leader of an influential new literary movement. *Les Soirées de Médan*, a group of short stories by the major naturalist writers which served as a kind of collective affirmation of Zola's program, came out in 1880.[9] But after this, the movement began to break up. Maupassant began to write psychological novels and Huysmans published the much-acclaimed symbolist novel *À Rebours* in 1884. Zola, as the only one to whom naturalism had brought success, found himself relatively isolated personally, and placed in the paradoxical position of being almost the sole visible representative of an enterprise which had been founded on the notion of collaboration.

The situation of Zola at this time, then, gives reason for supposing that *L'Œuvre* should be regarded at one level as a defense, and that its preoccupation with the status of the individual in the milieu of art responds to developments which cast the author, against his will, in the role of a solitary *grand homme* deserted by his earlier followers. Those who remained loyal to naturalism, like Paul Alexis, were precisely the ones who did not make a name for themselves.[10] Zola's commercial and public success was accompanied by the dissolution of the collective basis which would have vindicated it as the triumph of a modern art beyond the limits of romantic individualism.

L'Œuvre directly engages the question of the relationship between the founding of a revolutionary program and the nature of genius and success. But it does so within an almost entirely artistic context: the only writer in the novel, apart from the art critic, Jory, is Pierre Sandoz, a novelist whom Zola based on himself. It is true that Zola was familiar with the world of art: he knew many artists personally, grew up with Cézanne, met regularly with a group of them in the Café Guerbois, wrote influential articles on Cézanne and Manet. But the *soirées de Médan*, Sandoz' "jeudis" in the novel, were specifically literary gatherings in real life: for Zola, the parallel to the *bande* of *L'Œuvre* was the original group of naturalist writers. The effect of this displacement or simplification is to focus the area of conflict into a domain other than that of literature. Sandoz has neither colleagues nor rivals: he is simply a steady producer and theorist.

The fields of art and literature at the time did have much in common – not only anecdotally, in the friendships between their participants and the exchange of ideas, but also in wider social conditions relating to the production and practice of the arts. But literature was subject to certain changes which did not apply to the *beaux-arts*. The huge expansion of the reading public and the expansion in output of readable matter made *la lecture à la portée de tous*, "reading for all," a feasible program. As chapter 6 pointed out, cheap *quotidiens* and magazines had circulations of hundreds of thousands by the 1880s. Reading was another instance of "the democratization of luxury": no longer an elegant privilege but a new consumer industry. The Goncourts and others regularly complained, as had Sainte-Beuve at an earlier stage, of the "industrialization" of the novel, the genre best adapted to develop with the new conditions and even to be integrated into newspapers in the form of the *roman-feuilleton*.

The conflict perceived between artistic and commercial

values was translated at the level of theory into the unprecedented formulation of "art for art's sake," *l'art pour l'art*. In literature, the locus of this isolation was poetry, a genre without mass appeal. Its exclusive readership and its dissociation, as a result, from market considerations, tended to attract writers from a superior social background who did not depend on literature as a means of support, a contrast evident from comparisons of the Parnassian and symbolist poets with the novelists of the same period.[11] The extension of the market for literature is thus reflected in a bifurcation, along conventional social lines, of both consumers and producers, and a parallel reorientation of the relationship between different genres in accordance with this division.

Zola's earlier essay on "L'Argent et la littérature"[12] is ostensibly a vindication of the new commercial conditions of literary production, which imply a liberation for the writer from the old-fashioned dependence of art on the chances of patronage. "The book, which used to be a luxury object, has now become an object of routine consumption,"[13] and from this democratization of the market develops a juster, more meritocratic system:

> The writer is granted new means of existence; and immediately the idea of hierarchy is no more, intelligence becomes a form of nobility, work acquires its own dignity. At the same time, it follows logically that the influence of the salons and the Academy disappears.[14]

But the broad outlines of this historical trajectory, from luxury to general consumption and from patronage to professionalism, can also be translated into the polemics and divisions of the contemporary situation. Zola alludes to this only by the hint that his essay is an answer to those who continually protest against the invasion of literature by commerce on the grounds that "money kills the spirit."[15]

Unlike Gissing, who looks back to a comforting bygone world where literature and a hierarchical society were eternally one, Zola welcomes with open arms the modern order which is making literature part of the widespread commercial order from which the English writer withdraws. But he also, paradoxically, assumes that valuation of literature which rates it, whether for conservative or revolutionary ends, precisely by its distance from the ephemera of "routine consumption." For the essay is not arguing for the disappearance of the individual artist in favor of the mere professional or wage-earner. Zola is against state subsidies to artists because they only promote mediocrity, whereas the market provides an open field for the creator to make his way:

> Books and plays are not objects of routine consumption like for instance hats and shoes . . . . No, in all this it is genius alone which matters. There is no excuse for subsidies . . .
>
> It is only necessary to let things take their course, since talent cannot be dispensed to anyone and talent, appropriately enough, brings with it adequate power for its complete development.[16]

Génie, talent, essential value remain as independent criteria. Yet their realization and recognition somehow occur mechanically, through the discrimination – "laisser aller," unspecified in form or agency – of the competitive, value-free system to which their "power" is directed:

> The great law of life is struggle, you are owed nothing, you are bound to triumph if you are a force . . . . Therefore have respect for money, do not fall into that infantile habit of railing against it like poets.[17]

The euphoric confidence of these claims has no place in the lost illusions of the world depicted in *L'Œuvre*, where the "incomplete genius"[18] of Claude Lantier makes no impression on either the classical conservatism of the annual Salon juries, or the uncomprehending public. Claude's adamant opposition to "ce bas intérêt de commerce" (III, 130) and his scorn for common stupidity, "la bêtise publique" (II, 100), are marked, it is true, as being signs of his general "impuissance," the incapacity to adapt which causes his family's near starvation. He has the arrogant aestheticism of "absolute disdain for everything other than painting" (II, 99).[19] But there remains the basic question as to why the revolutionary genius of Claude's work is never granted by the public, at the same time that it becomes the unacknowledged foundation of a host of popularizing and commercial imitators. The differing attitudes and survival strategies of the other members of the band put Claude's failure into perspective, and the relationships that emerge between the interrelationships of commerce, genius, old and new orders, are far more complex in the 1886 novel than those of the earlier manifesto.

The fifteen-year timespan of the novel, and the recurrent allusions to the youthful country rambles shared by Sandoz, Lantier and the architect Dubuche in Plassans, provide Zola with a historical perspective which in some ways appears as the reverse of the optimistic movement sketched out in "L'Argent." In the beginning, the artistic revolution Claude envisages is described as a triumph over stale academic formulae:

> Was there anything else in art than giving forth what you had in your guts? . . . Wasn't a bunch of carrots, yes, a bunch of carrots! directly observed and naively painted with the personal touch through which you saw it, worth the same as the eternal confections of the École, that tobacco juice painting shamefully cooked according to the recipes? (II, 100)[20]

But the novel traces a negative passage from youth to age, from idealism to disillusion, from the provinces to Paris, and from camaraderie to rivalry. It is crystallized in the story of Claude, whose early "ambition of desiring to see everything, do everything, conquer everything" (VIII, 261)[21] is soured into perpetual inability, in the terms of Zola's essay, to bring his genius to fulfillment.

The relatively simple case of genius corrupted either by inherent weakness, or by the adverse effects of an environment that does not recognize it, is complicated by the fact that at the end of the novel, Claude's revolution has been accomplished without him: without the *chef d'œuvre* he never achieves. At the last reunion of the original *bande*, Gagnière, the second-rate landscape painter, complains that his own work is always identified with Claude's:

> He's completely stolen my originality from me! Do you think it amuses me to have heard the same thing repeated behind my back with each painting, these past fifteen years: "It's a Claude!" (XI, 391)[22]

When Sandoz runs into Claude at the Salon where the latter's *Enfant mort* has gone unnoticed, he consoles him against the public indifference which seems worse to the painter than ridicule:

> "Everyone imitates you now, ever since your *Open Air* which they laughed at so much . . . Look, look! . . . " With his hand, across the galleries, he pointed out canvases. Sure enough, the stroke of clarity gradually introduced into contemporary painting was finally bursting forth . . . The old academic subjects had taken their leave, along with the reboiled juices of tradition.
> "Ah! your part is still a fine one, old chap!" continued Sandoz. "The art of tomorrow will be yours, you have made them all." (X, 354-5)[23]

Claude's uniqueness has been generalized into the familiar type of "un Claude" and the rawness of his revolutionary "carottes" has been garnished and refined into a recipe tasteful to the modern Salon.

In this light, the artist Fagerolles can be seen as the real fulfillment of Claude, the man who succeeds in translating the roughness of Claude's approaches into a final and palatable form. The iconoclastic reputation of the "Plein air" school becomes an actual advantage for one whose work is similar but less challenging:

> He profited from all the hatred people had of them, his mollified canvases were showered with praise in order to kill the stubbornly violent works of the others. (VII, 252)[24]

And Fagerolles' success at the Salon where Claude exhibits the *Enfant mort* modeled on his own dead son, is nothing but a softened version of the painting of Claude's which was laughed down at the Salon des Refusés several years before:[25]

> It was Fagerolles' painting. And he saw again his *Open Air* in this *Picnic*, the same sunlight effect, the same artistic principles, but so toned down, so faked, so spoilt, with its superficial elegance composed with infinite consideration for the vulgar satisfactions of the public. (X, 345)[26]

In the moral terms of the novel, Fagerolles is a traitor or thief, "le malin des malins" (VI, 221). But he is also the midwife who produces in a living, socially adapted form what Claude has "dans le ventre" and could bring forth only as his dead child. And in the same way, while Fagerolles personally is an ambitious egoist ruled by "la démangeaison du succès" (VI, 221), his *oeuvre* represents the birth of a new order in which the artist is made not by rudimentary, inherent genius but by flexibility and the capacity to adjust to given conditions. Where Claude fails, Fagerolles becomes "the one who would embody the formula in masterpieces," and his work stands in relation to Claude's not as copy to original but as finished product to raw material: he is the chef who transforms the revolutionary fodder. This conversion of primary materials into a marketable commodity makes the relation of the two painters into more than a personal history: it is a paradigmatic tale of the changes in the social determinations of art that were going on at the time.

The commercial developments are pointed succinctly by the contrast of the two dealers in the novel, Malgras and Naudet. The first is presented as a conventional type of wily tradesman, without social graces but adept at minor dissimulation in the business of buying the work of a struggling young artist at bargain rates. But this "primitive trickery, for getting hold of the canvas he was after at a low price" (II, 110)[27] is accompanied by a real appreciation and love of the art, a "jouissance de connaisseur" (II, 110). He knows a masterpiece when he sees one, and his haggling is based on a solid assurance of genuine worth, in which monetary and artistic values are related: it is the outstanding painting which will fetch the highest price when he resells it.

Naudet, on the other hand, is a smooth financier concerned with the qualities of the paintings he sells only in so far as they represent potential dividends:

> A speculator, a wheeler-dealer . . . he figured out which artist to launch, not the one who promised to become a master painter of widely discussed genius, but the one whose deceptive talent . . . would sell at a high price on the bourgeois market. And it was in this way that he was completely turning the market upside down, by pushing aside the old-fashioned, discriminating amateur who knows nothing about art and buys a picture like a share on the market – out of vanity, or hoping that it will rise in value. (VII, 243)[28]

The man who "révolutionnait le commerce des tableaux" (VII, 243) is as much an iconoclast as Claude. But while Claude responds to the failure of his revolution by the futile smashing of his actual canvases, Naudet's successful one involves, ironically, a complete break with the materiality of art, whose visual and physical qualities cease to matter. His *tableaux* are transformed into purely monetary values – luxury investments to be sold to characters like "un marchand de porcs de New York" (XI, 387),[29] or sold in "les grands magasins modernes de l'art" (X, 348). The picture becomes nothing more than a commodity, an arbitrary bearer of the value ascribed to it by the market; the artists who work for him are "a fine generation of derivative painters doubling as dishonest businessmen" (VII, 244).[30] Naudet's business has no place for stable, specifically aesthetic value in the work of art, but only for the ever-increasing turnover of profit-making exchange, "le mouvement fou qui était son œuvre" (XI, 387).

As with any other kind of commodity, the arbitrary value of

this new-style work of art has to be given a social basis of plausibility, and *L'Œuvre* describes in detail the media and institutions supporting Naudet and epitomized in the figure of Jory, the journalist of the original group who, from the beginning, "had made himself an art critic" (III, 126). Where Sandoz can claim that Claude "made" the new generation of painters, in another and equally significant sense it is the promotional efforts of Jory who, through his deployment of the critical media at his disposal, "claimed to have made Fagerolles, as he claimed previously to have made Claude" (VII, 252).

Bongrand, the older master who associates with the *Plein air* group, declaims against the modern "trompettes de la publicité" in art:

> And what publicity! an uproar from one end of France to the other, sudden reputations that spring up overnight and burst out in claps of thunder in the midst of the gaping populace. Not to mention the works, those pathetic works heralded with gun salutes, awaited in a frenzy of anticipation, driving Paris wild for a week and then sinking into eternal oblivion. (VII, 241-2)[31]

Art in its commodified form thus retains its appeal to the spectator by means of this new, systematic production of ephemeral values: the mass media give it a marketable image. By a parallel shift, the artist is provided with all the allure of a modern celebrity. Fagerolles, "tambouriné, affiché, célebré" (IX, 314), is promoted with all the force of "ce coup brutal de la publicité," which gives information as to the distinctive personality of its object as particular as the number of eggs he eats for breakfast (X, 349).

L'Œuvre thus offers strong reservations about the simplicity of the encounter between genius and the market evoked in the essay on money and literature. The new commerce, with its accompanying promotional system, is a third element which intervenes to overthrow the residual criteria of authentic value, arbitrarily creating its stars and its masterworks by processes of valorization which do not distinguish between a Claude and a

Fagerolles as raw material. But once again, it would be a mistake to suppose that Zola here simply replaces the dichotomy between old-fashioned patronage and modern money-based meritocracy by one which opposes balanced to overdeveloped commercial systems. Zola, after all, spent three years as "chef de publicité" for the Hachette publishing house; as a journalist, he wrote articles influential in forming new trends in art and literature; *L'Œuvre* itself, finally, is among other things an inside scoop on the private lives of Bohemia.

The novel never explicitly holds external determinations responsible for Claude's lack of achievement; in fact, the period of his youthful arrogance and optimism is characterized as "a wilful ignorance of the necessities of social life" (III, 129). The complete genius is not a raw, asocial force, but a talent able to adapt to and, to a limited extent, to adapt the milieu he finds himself in. In this context, the various explanations of Claude's weakness – hereditary flaw, residual romanticism, childish disposition – become so many pointers at the individual level to the social and historical anachronism he represents.

One practical effect of writing about the artistic rather than the literary world was that it enabled Zola to place the questions of originality and imitation, revolutionary and market forces, in a sharper focus. In relation to literature, painting was itself an anachronistic art, dealing in the unique and potentially priceless object rather than the infinitely reproducible copies in which the literary *œuvre* was distributed. The expansion of printed matter, which Zola identifies as a positive, democratic development in "L'Argent et la littérature," has no direct artistic counterpart. But there were other innovations which marginalized the role of the traditional painter. Claude's declared "dream, to cover the walls of Paris" (XI, 389) draws attention to the fact that he is not painting posters. And ironically, the graves in the cemetery where he is buried at the end of the novel are adorned with an assortment of modern mementoes, "including even photographs of women, cheap yellow photographs" (XII, 415).

Claude is not of his time; but among the group which includes such tricky manipulators of the modern system as Jory and Fagerolles is one who is neither insincere nor old-fashioned: the novelist. Sandoz' success is mentioned rather than stressed, and his work is generally represented as the cumulative and continual effort of an *ouvrier* rather than as the all-or-nothing struggle of a perfectionist:

> The writer had just published a new novel; and although the critics were not letting up, with this one he was all the same making himself the kind of reputation which consecrates a man, however persistent his opponents' attacks. He had, moreover, no illusions, well aware that the battle he had won would begin again with every one of his books. The great work of his life was advancing, this series of novels, these volumes he was launching blow by blow with determined regularity, proceeding towards the goal he had set himself without letting himself be conquered by anything – obstacles, injuries or fatigue. (XI, 382)[32]

The regular, methodical production of *nulla dies sine linea* can, all the same, carry with it a form of madness which makes it not necessarily preferable to Claude's inability to finish anything. Sandoz at one point bursts out in a long complaint against his subjugation to the unrelenting obligations of production:

> "Listen, work has taken over my existence . . . Nothing, nothing in my hole any more but work and me . . .!" (IX, 320)[33]

In the *Ébauche*, Zola says explicitly that the account of Claude's method of work is as much his own as that of Sandoz: together they will make up "toute ma confession," "toute ma vie intime de production" (*Ébauche*, fols. 261, 287). The words which follow the second phrase are, however, underlined to mark the relative place of Sandoz as "<u>Un echo pratique et résigné de Claude</u>" (*Ébauche*, fols. 287-8).

Sandoz' work is not discussed in regard to its quality: the oppositions of originality and derivativeness, genius and fulfillment are not mentioned in relation to the writer. This difference from the debates about art is naturalized in the novel by the absence of literary colleagues and competitors for Sandoz, who only associates with his artist friends. But in light of the crisis situation of naturalism as a program in the mid-1880s, and Zola as its increasingly isolated, though publicly successful, representative, it can be interpreted as a plea for the novel as a middle way beyond the now futile opposition between Romantic genius and market mediocrity; between art as aesthetic and art as a modern consumer industry.

Sandoz himself is socially an example of the new professional middle class; the increasing income from his work goes towards the material development of a thoroughly conventional bourgeois home, which is contrasted to the downward trend of Claude's domestic situation and the excesses of Fagerolles' palatial surroundings:

> The sales of his books were increasing and making him rich; the rue de Londres apartment was becoming most luxurious compared with the little bourgeois home in the Batignolles; and he remained just the same. (XI, 380)[34]

The bourgeois moderation and financial solidity of the literary producer is in perfect correspondence to the median position of the serious novel-reading public half-way between the aesthetes and the masses, as described by Christophe Charle.[35]

Between the absolute, unique qualities of the master and the inflated pseudo-values of Jory's "jolie génération" of second-rate celebrities, there remains the sanity of "la tâche quotidienne." It is the oppressive but indispensable discipline of an artistic project fitted to the short-term, continual requirements of the modern market, with the eventual accumulation of "des livres sur des livres, l'entassement d'une montagne" (IX, 321). Unlike Claude, "toujours en bataille avec le réel" (IX, 303), Sandoz' naturalism is a means of control against the destructive "sauce romantique" (II, 103):

> "Our generation is too clogged in lyricism to leave works of

sanity . . . Truth, nature, this is the only possible basis, the necessary police outside of which madness begins; and there need be no fear of flattening the work, for temperament will always be there to dominate the creator. (XII, 416)[36]

What he seeks is the demarcation of a workable boundary between reason and madness, and the displacement of notions of timeless quality by serial progression and quantitative accretion. These aims are realized in the restricted contract which Sandoz undertakes for himself:

"I've found what I needed for myself. Oh, not much – just a little corner, something sufficient for a human life." (VI, 219-20)[37]

Thus the project of the Rougon-Macquart novels, the squarely bounded "coin" or "morceau" of a moderate professional ambition adapted to the conditions of "une période historique déterminée," functions as the logical resolution of the post-Romantic dilemma: not a scattering of brilliant poetic fragments, but an ordered sequence of measurable parts. Sandoz, realizing that he is losing his morning's work, hurries away from the grave of a Claude who could not escape from "la gangrène romantique," with the words which end the work: "Allons travailler," "To work!"

Postscript

In the six novels discussed above, subjective identity and conceptions of art are always mediated, explicitly or not, by the thorough commodification which characterizes urban society at the turn of the century. For Gissing, the demands of a competitive, monetary economy are superimposed upon what would ideally be a free and creative artistic self, and thus the embittered but futile resistance of those who sense the contradiction is contrasted with the easy capitulations of the efficient professional man or stupidly contented woman. In Dreiser's writing, commodification has a wholly attractive appearance, the endless and dreamlike promise of the advertisement. Commercial and artistic values not only are not but should not be separated. The successful artist or adman is as much of a fashion-conscious consumer as the woman, but whereas she figures passively as an image of youthful perfection or of a Broadway star, he represents the force of an entrepreneur. Zola analyzes contemporary forms in terms of how they differ from those of the recent past and he neither condemns nor celebrates – or else does both: his department store is both a fantasy palace and an oppressive machine. This neutrality is itself a function of the professionalism he sees as the only workable possibility for the modern writer in a market system where individuals have no power.

Such an accommodation was barely accessible to women at the time. An Edith Wharton, with independent means of support, might establish herself as a critic of New York aristocratic life from within, or a Mrs Frank Leslie acquire both money and stardom through her literary and journalistic enterprises.[1] In general, though, intellectual achievement on the part of women was accompanied by a conscious refusal of the trappings of femininity. Professional women, like Rhoda Nunn in Gissing's *The Odd Women* (1893), could only establish their credentials for seriousness by distancing themselves from the frivolous indulgence associated with their sex. H.G. Wells summarized his novel *Marriage* (1916) as "how masculine intellectual interest met feminine spending and what ensued."[2] This points to the problem: while a "masculine" head might accommodate spending interests – become a controlled consumer and still be regarded as a rational person – the woman, identified primarily as irrational, excessive "feminine spending," could less easily gain access to what was perceived as the life of the mind. Rational and analytical or aesthetic and pleasurable modes remained for her rigid alternatives, and for the most part therefore it was men at this time who studied the relations between the two in ways defined as objective such as the naturalist novel. Which is also to say that claiming their "overviews" as objective and scientific by comparison with popular sentimental or sensational products, naturalist novelists were able to legitimate their enterprise as properly masculine.

The discussion of consumer culture at the turn of the century could be extended to literary forms other than naturalist novels in which it is overtly thematized. Rosalind H. Williams, for instance, shows how J.-K. Huysmans' reclusive aesthete hero Des Esseintes is in fact an exemplary consumer in spite of his

---

Illustration 13   Still looking?

apparent withdrawal from the world.[3] In another reversal of received aesthetic sensibilities, Jean-Christophe Agnew has brilliantly dissected the "consuming vision" of Henry James.[4] Similarly, the Wildean aesthete continually making and remaking artistic poses and identities, as in *The Picture of Dorian Gray* (1890), reveals the profound connection at this time between the values and images of "pure" art and those of fashion. Not just looking, but looking at looking as the dominant mode of experience for artists and consumers alike, the naturalists bring into focus Wilde's suitably visual definition: "It is the spectator, and not life, that art really mirrors."[5]

Notes

Chapter 1

1 "Europe is on the move to look at merchandise." Quoted in Benjamin, *Reflections*, p. 151.
2 See *La Société du Spectacle*.
3 "Il semble que la vente engendre la vente, et que les objets les plus dissemblables, ainsi juxtaposés, se prêtent un mutuel appui." ("Le mécanisme de la vie moderne," p. 356).
4 Some of the roots of the commercialization of everyday life are described in McKendrick, Brewer and Plumb, *The Birth of a Consumer Society: the Commercialization of Eighteenth-Century England*. The differences are in terms of scale and systematization. Fashion, for instance, was not itself new in the nineteenth century, but its social significance was now overwhelmingly extended as it became an organized industry catering to a middle-class market and producing standardized ready-made garments following the invention of the sewing machine in the early 1850s.
5 Which is not to imply that the fantasies of films and of displays of goods do not themselves become a new kind of necessity – or that the notion of necessity has no meaning, as opposed to a stable reference, in an expanding consumer economy.

6   See Bok, "Literary factories."

7   *Reflections*, p. 157. The arcades, architectural precursors of the domed department stores, were glass-topped passages flanked by small boutiques. Benjamin's writings are a rich source of insights and suggestions regarding the nineteenth-century city and the effects on art of commercial and technological changes. This quotation comes from "Paris, Capital of the Nineteenth Century," his exposé for a book on the arcades, partially completed in 1940 when he died, and published now in vol. V of the *Gesammelte Schriften*. Three collections of his essays (with some overlapping) are available in English: *Illuminations, One-Way Street and Other Writings* and *Reflections*.

8   *Writer and Critic*, p. 144.

9   Lukács mentions the new market conditions for authors, who had now become "specialists in the craft of writing in the sense of the capitalist division of labour. The book had become merchandise, the writer, a salesman of this merchandise" (p. 119).

10 See Benjamin's seminal essay, "The work of art in the age of mechanical reproduction," in *Illuminations*, pp. 217-51.

11 "Une nouvelle façon de concevoir les rapports de la littérature à la société"; "Toujours est-il que le naturalisme témoigne d'une incontestable propension à rompre les cadres contraignants" (*Le Naturalisme*, pp. 92, 93).

12 "Preface to Shakespeare" (1765), in Cruttwell (ed.), *Selected Writings*, Harmondsworth, Penguin, 1968, p. 263.

13 In Joyce's *Ulysses*, Stephen Dedalus combines the object before him with a version of a Wildean aphorism to suggest a symbol for Irish art in "the cracked looking glass of a servant." For naturalism, too, the smooth surface of realism must be cracked, so that reality and the mirror appear warps and all. The mirror with its cracks reveals itself as a mirror, and reveals a world itself made up of mirrors and images.

14 Its associations of seriousness are perhaps one reason why naturalism was a form more available to male writers of the time, attractive in its seeming distance from more trivially "feminine" ways of looking and of writing. See Chapter 8.

15 *The World a Department Store*, the title of Bradford Peck's novel, published at his own expense in 1900, takes this to the limit. It consists of a guided tour through a bland, saccharine and utterly

novel "Christian capitalist co-operative" utopia, realized in the New England of the future 1920s.

16 See, for instance, Hemmings, *Émile Zola*; Ripoll, *Réalité et mythe chez Zola*.

17 Relevant works include the papers from the 1976 Colloque de Cerisy collected in *Le Naturalisme*; Sundquist (ed.) *American Realism: New Essays*. In addition to a chapter in Jameson's *The Political Unconscious: Narrative as a Socially Symbolic Act*, Gissing has been well served by Goode's *George Gissing: Ideology and Fiction* and Poole's *Gissing in Context*.

Chapter 2

1 *Captains of Consciousness: Advertising and the Social Roots of the Consumer Culture*.

2 For further information see Chirot, *Social Change in the Twentieth Century*. Accounts of the development of consumer capitalism in each country can be found in Davis, *A History of Shopping*; Jones, *The Consumer Society: A History of American Capitalism*; Thil, *Les Inventeurs du commerce moderne*.

3 Quoted in Wendt and Kogan, *Give the Lady What She Wants*, p. 29.

4 In addition, the proliferation of gadgets marketed for the speedier performance of previously undreamt-of culinary complexities or household chores can be seen as an effective abolition of the distinction between necessary and superfluous domestic tasks.

5 *Women's Oppression Today: Problems in Marxist Feminist Analysis*.

6 *Capital*, vol. I.

7 ibid., pp. 142–3.

8 See in particular his *Le Système des objets* and *La Société de consommation*.

9 *The Image: A Guide to Pseudo-Events in America*.

10 "Il faut se garder d'interpréter cette gigantesque entreprise de production d'artefact, de make-up, de pseudo-objets, de pseudo-événements qui envahit notre existence quotidienne comme dénaturation ou falsification d'un 'contenu' authentique . . . C'est dans la forme que tout a changé: il y a partout substitution, en lieu et place du réel, d'un 'néo-réel' tout entier produit à partir des éléments du code." (*La Société*, p. 195).

11 "Chacun se doit d'être 'au courant', et de se recycler annuelle-
ment, mensuellement, saisonnièrement dans ses vêtements, ses
objets, sa voiture. S'il ne le fait, il n'est pas un vrai citoyen de la
société de consommation" (ibid., p. 149).

12 *Capital*, p. 178.

13 On the semiotics of fashion, see Barthes, *Système de la Mode*.
Virginia Woolf has a witty section on spectacular male uniforms
in the church, the army and the lawcourts in *Three Guineas*.

14 On the social effects of photography and its offshoots, see Benjamin, "A short history of photography."

15 The intention here is not to debate the vexed question of how far
Freud's theories can be applied to periods other than his own,
but to place his preoccupation with questions of pleasure, subjectivity and gender identity in the context of some other contemporary discourses and social forms.

16 See in particular "On Narcissism: An Introduction" (1914), vol.
XIV, pp. 73-102. Key texts on the development of femininity
are: "Some Psychical Consequences of the Anatomical Distinction Between the Sexes" (1925), vol. XIX; "Female Sexuality"
(1931), vol. XXI and "Femininity" (1933), vol. XXII.

17 The reading given here is mediated by Lacan's early essay, translated as "The Mirror Stage as formative of the function of the I"
in *Écrits*, pp. 1–7. Psychoanalytic accounts concentrate on the
determining effects of general cultural structures and early
family relationships rather than on the way that particular
sociohistorical forms inflect the shape of early and later
experiences. The concern here is to look at mirrors of identification and separation other than, though related to, those that the
baby sees: to suggest how available imaginary identifications in
the late nineteenth century were open to historically new forms
of (ad)dress or *interpellation*, to use Louis Althusser's term.

18 It was assuredly no accident when British suffragettes spent the
afternoon of 1 March 1912 systematically smashing the windows
of famous London stores such as Liberty's, Marshall and
Snelgrove, and Swan and Edgar. Signifying possibly irreparable
cracks in bourgeois ideology, "the argument of the broken window
pane," as George Dangerfield put it, quite properly appeared to
the man in the street as rather "unseemly outbreaks." See
Dangerfield, *The Strange Death of Liberal England*.

158

Notes

Chapter 3

1 See in particular Halperin, *Gissing: A Life in Books*; Korg, *George Gissing: A Critical Biography*; Tindall, *The Born Exile: George Gissing*.

2 Gissing, *Eve's Ransom* (1895), repr. New York, Dover, 1980, ch. IV, p. 19. All further references appear in the text.

3 The most obvious parallels are Henry Ryecroft (*The Private Papers of Henry Ryecroft*), Godwin Peak (*Born in Exile*) and Hugh Kingscote (*Isabel Clarendon*). Intellectuals in Gissing are rarely integrated members of a community (Sidney Kirkwood of *The Nether World* is one exception; so too Gilbert Grail of *Thyrza*, a self-taught working man without ambition but also without many friends). The futility of some, but not enough, education, is a frequent theme. Gissing was opposed to the minimal elementary education requirement brought in by the 1870 Education Act, and there are a number of unfavorable portraits of under-educated leaders or scholars (Hugh Mutimer, the working-class leader of *Demos*; Luke Ackroyd in *The Nether World*). The divorce between mental and manual work, discussed in the chapter on *New Grub Street*, often arises as a question of social snobbery and the impossibility for a man of middle-class origins of engaging in wage labor or "trade." *Will Warburton* features an intellectual unwillingly and shamefully turned grocer, for whom respectability is restored by the perfect compromise of a small bookstore – trade, but trade of a fairly eccentric and thus more socially legitimate sort. Similarly, in *The Whirlpool*, a gentleman disillusioned with the tangles and scandals of high society finance finds peace of mind in the steadiness of running a photography shop.

4 Tindall relates the proliferation of "unexpected legacies" in Gissing's fiction to "the typical novelist's ignorance about how finance actually works" (*The Born Exile*, pp. 34-5).

5 *Standard Edition*, vol. XXII, p. 113.

6 It was during the last part of the nineteenth century that the social sciences took their modern disciplinary form. See Abrams, *The Origins of British Sociology*.

7 The combination of attraction and repulsion in relation to modern life is characteristic of Matthew Arnold's writing, which has

similar thematic preoccupations to Gissing's in regard to the idea of culture. Like Hilliard, Arnold consistently maintains an opposition between "machinery," the grim actuality of modern life, and the timeless, harmonious values of the Greek world. See in particular *Culture and Anarchy* (1869).

Chapter 4

1 Dreiser, *Sister Carrie*, Philadelphia, University of Pennsylvania Press, 1981, p. 78. All further quotations will appear within the text; pagination is the same in the Penguin edition, also of 1981. This new text restores what Dreiser wrote prior to the revisions and cuts made mostly by others for the first edition, published in 1900.

2 The Fair was less prestigious in Chicago than its chief rival, Marshall Field, whose history is written in Wendt and Kogan's *Give the Lady What She Wants*. Chicago was also at this time the center of the rapidly expanding mail-order enterprises of Montgomery Ward and Sears, Roebuck: it was through their extensively illustrated catalogues that inhabitants of rural areas like Carrie would see their first images of urban consumer abundance. General accounts of American shopping during the Gilded Age are to be found in Barth, *City People*, ch. V, and Trachtenberg, *The Incorporation of America: Culture and Society in the Gilded Age*, pp. 130-9.

3 Jameson discusses a similar passage on Carrie's fascination with the commodified attractions of the city: "For all the caressing solicitations of this text, it clearly positions us outside Carrie's desire, which is represented as a private wish or longing to which we relate . . . by the mechanisms of identification and projection, and to which we may also adopt a moralizing stance, or what amounts to the same thing, an ironic one" (*The Political Unconscious*, p. 160). Thus "the tawdriness of Carrie's hunger for trinkets, a tawdriness that Dreiser's language ambiguously represents and reflects all at once" (p. 159) is as it were both advertised and set at a distance: a mirror made visible for what it is.

4 "*Sister Carrie*'s popular economy."

5 ibid., p. 381.

6 ibid., p. 390.

Notes

7 The rapid expansion and relative popularization of urban leisure industries at this time, from dining out to music and shows, then the cinema, is described by Erenberg in *Steppin' Out: New York Nightlife and the Transformation of American Culture 1890-1930*.

8 Carrie's position is much the same as that of the early movie stars, who took over the pinnacles of public visibility in the period immediately after the publication of Dreiser's novel. The phenomenon of the star as both inaccessible image and focus of public identification is discussed in Dyer's *Stars*, and Morin, *Les Stars*.

9 Mallarmé, who like Dreiser at one time edited a ladies' fashion magazine, makes the same point to his readers: "Everything is learned from life, even beauty, and the carriage of the head is taken from someone, which is to say from everyone, like the way to wear a dress." ("Tout s'apprend sur le vif, même la beauté, et le port de tête, on le tient de quelqu'un, c'est-à-dire de chacun, comme le port d'une robe.") *La Dernière Mode* (1874), in *Œuvres Complètes*, ed. Henri Mondor and G. Jean-Aubry, Paris, Gallimard, coll. Pléiade, 1945, p. 617.

10 "The language of realism, the language of false consciousness."

11 ibid., p. 109.

12 ibid., p. 107.

13 In Dreiser's novels, there is no clear-cut distinction between the sexes with regard to their constitution as fashion-conscious consumer subjects: Hurstwood and the "butterfly" Drouet are as much concerned with a public image guaranteed by clothes of a certain style as Carrie herself. In this respect, Dreiser's world is closer to that of present-day consumer society, where fashion is not perceived and projected as an exclusively feminine concern to the same extent as it was in 1900, and where clothing styles themselves are not rigidly identified with one sex or the other.

Chapter 5

1 The other store was the Louvre, now closed.

2 *The Bon Marché: Bourgeois Culture and the Department Store*.

3 Chapter II, p. 80. Page numbers are taken from Colette Becker's edition, Paris, Garnier Flammarion, 1971. All further references appear within the text.

4   Sennett discusses the effects of the abandonment of specific dress tied to social class following the Revolution of 1789 in *The Fall of Public Man*.

5   *Dream Worlds: Mass Consumption in Late Nineteenth-Century France*.

6   ibid., pp. 398, 401.

7   Boucicaut took over the Bon Marché in 1852, and the period of rapid expansion that is going on at the start of Zola's novel corresponds to the 1860s in the store's history. But for the day-to-day running of the enterprise, Zola's account is based on the researches he did at the Bon Marché and the Louvre prior to writing the book during 1882 (it was published in 1883).

8   This global penetration, based on the practices at the Bon Marché, has a parallel in the big American mail-order houses such as Sears Roebuck, whose catalogues put outlying rural areas in touch with one another. See Boorstin, *The Americans: The Democratic Experience*; also pages reproduced from Montgomery Ward catalogue in this volume, pp. 55–7.

9   "Un bien-être les envahissait, il leur semblait entrer dans le printemps, au sortir de l'hiver de la rue. Tandis que, dehors, soufflait le vent glacé des giboulées, déjà la belle saison, dans les galeries du *Bonheur*, s'attiédissait avec les étoffes légères, l'éclat fleuri des nuances tendres, la gaieté champêtre des modes d'été et des ombrelles."

10 "Ils avaient éveillé dans sa chair de nouveaux désirs, ils étaient une tentation immense, où elle succombait fatalement, cédant d'abord à des achats de bonne ménagère, puis gagnée par la coquetterie, puis dévorée."

11 "La femme venait passer chez lui les heures vides, les heures frissonnantes et inquiètes qu'elle vivait jadis au fond des chapelles: dépense nécessaire de passion nerveuse, lutte renaissante d'un dieu contre le mari, culte sans cesse renouvelé du corps, avec l'au-delà divin de la beauté."

12 "Partout les glaces reculaient les magasins, reflétaient des étalages avec des coins de public, des visages renversés, des moités d'épaules et de bras."

13 "Et, en bas, ainsi que dans une vasque, dormaient les étoffes lourdes, les armures façonnées, les damas, les brocarts, les soies perlées et lamées, au milieu d'un lit profond de velours, tous les

velours, noirs, blancs, de couleur, frappés à fond de soie ou de satin, creusant avec leurs taches mouvantes un lac immobile où semblaient danser des reflets de ciel et de paysage. Des femmes, pâles de désir, se penchaient comme pour se voir. Toutes, en face de cette cataracte lâchée, restaient debout, avec la peur sourde d'être prises dans le débordement d'un pareil luxe et avec l'irrésistible envie de s'y jeter et de s'y perdre."

14 The inverse process can also occur when advertising billboards take their place in the natural landscape. The *Bon Marché* appointments diary for 1915 carried a series of full-page cartoon drawings showing the naturalization of the store into the urban and rural landscape by means of posters which serve some useful function: one provides shade at a picnic, another causes motorists to slow down before a dangerous bend, and so on.

15 It is worth stressing the double meaning of the French word, in which "consumption" and "consummation," shopping and sex are joined together.

16 "Mouret avait l'unique passion de vaincre la femme. Il la voulait reine dans sa maison; il lui avait bâti ce temple, pour l'y tenir à sa merci. C'était toute sa tactique, la griser d'attentions galantes et trafiquer de ses désirs, exploiter sa fièvre. Aussi, nuit et jour, se creusait-il la tête à la recherche de trouvailles nouvelles."

17 "Ce qu'il faut . . . c'est qu'elles se promènent pendant des heures, qu'elles se perdent. D'abord, elles auront l'air plus nombreuses. Ensuite . . . le magasin leur paraîtra plus grand. Enfin, c'est bien le diable si, errant dans ce désordre organisé, affolées, perdues, elles ne mettent pas les pieds dans des rayons où elles n'avaient pas l'intention d'aller, et si elles ne succombent pas à la vue d'articles qui les accrochent au passage." (Quoted in Thil, *Les Inventeurs du commerce moderne*, p. 34.)

18 "C'était la fin de la chair, un corps de fiancée usé dans l'attente, retourné à l'enfance, grêle des premiers ans. Lentement, Geneviève se recouvrit et elle répétait:- Vous voyez bien, je ne suis plus une femme."

19 Zola's notes for working conditions are extensive, and have themselves been used as a source for historical studies. In addition to *The Bon Marché*, two of the most useful studies are Parent-Lardeur, *Les Demoiselles de magasin*, and Lesselier, "Employées de grands magasins à Paris (avant 1914)."

20 The metaphors are used throughout the novel.

21 ["Ce mécanisme] créait entre les commis une lutte pour l'existence, dont les patrons bénéficiaient. Cette lutte devenait du reste entre ses mains la formule favorite, le principe d'organisation qu'il appliquait constamment. Il lâchait les passions, mettait les forces en présence, laissait les gros manger les petits, et s'engraissait de cette bataille des intérêts."

22 "Si la bataille continuelle de l'argent n'avait effacé les sexes, il aurait suffi, pour tuer le désir, de la bousculade de chaque minute . . . . Tous n'étaient plus que des rouages, se trouvaient emportés par le branle de la machine, abdiquant leur personnalité, additionnant simplement leurs forces." Cf. "C'était une lutte sourde, où elles-mêmes apportaient une égale âpreté; et, dans leur fatigue commune, toujours sur pied, la chair morte, les sexes disparaissaient, il ne restait plus face à face que des intérêts contraires, irrités par la fièvre du négoce" (It was a hidden struggle, in which the women themselves contributed an equal violence; and in their shared fatigue, always on their feet, their bodies exhausted, the sexes disappeared, there was nothing left between them but opposing interests, provoked by the feverish activity of the business) (IV, 143).

23 "Le pis était leur situation neutre, mal déterminée, entre la dame et la boutiquière. Ainsi jetées dans le luxe, souvent sans instruction première, elles formaient une classe à part, innommée."

24 – Qui est-ce?
– Oh! personne, répondit Mme. Desforges, de sa voix mauvaise. Une demoiselle de magasin qui attend.

25 Loss leaders are items sold at below cost price whose bargain quality is meant to encourage higher spending on other, more expensive products by lowering customers' resistance.

26 "Et, en quelques phrases dites à l'oreille du baron Hartmann, comme s'il eut fait de ces confidences amoureuses qui se risquent parfois entre hommes, [Octave] acheva d'expliquer le mécanisme du grand commerce moderne. Alors, plus haut que les faits déjà donnés apparut l'exploitation de la femme . . . . C'était la femme que les magasins se disputaient par la concurrence, la femme qu'ils prenaient au continuel piège de leurs occasions, après l'avoir étourdie devant leurs étalages."

27 As a sideline, Mouret's designs also produce new forms of madness,

notably kleptomania, "A perversion of desire, a new neurosis that an alienist [mental doctor] had classified in establishing the acute effects of the temptation produced by department stores" (IX, 277) ("une perversion du désir, une névrose nouvelle qu'un aliéniste avait classée, en y constatant le résultat aigu de la tentation exercée par les grands magasins"). There is also the sad case of M. Marty, rendered crazy by his wife's compulsive spending on fashion, "la folie dépensière de la mode" (XIV, 404): "Poor M. Marty, following violent domestic scenes, had just been afflicted with delusions of grandeur: he was digging up the treasures of the earth by handfuls, emptying gold mines, filling up carts with diamonds and precious stones" (XIV, 408) ("Le pauvre M. Marty, à la suite de violentes scènes de ménage, venait d'être frappé du délire des grandeurs: il puisait à pleines mains dans les trésors de la terre; il vidait les mines d'or, chargeait des tombereaux de diamants et de pierreries").

28 *Ébauche*, Bibliotheque Nationale, NAF ms. 10277, fol. 1.

Chapter 6

1 *Literature and Life*, pp. 268-9.
2 These general remarks apply equally to Britain, France and the United States. Factual information about authors and publishers used in this chapter is taken largely from Earl L. Bradsher, "Book publishers and publishing," in Trent *et al.* (eds), *The Cambridge History of American Literature*; Lough, *Writer and Public in France*; Sutherland, *Victorian Novelists and Publishers*; and Tebbel, *A History of Book Publishing in the United States, Vol. II: The Expansion of an Industry, 1865-1919*.
3 "On eut beau vouloir séparer dans le journal ce qui restait consciencieux et libre, de ce qui devenait public et vénal . . . Comment condamner à deux doigts de distance, qualifier détestable et funeste ce qui se proclamait et s'affichait deux doigts plus bas comme la merveille de l'époque? L'attraction des majuscules croissantes de l'annonce l'emporta: ce fut une montagne d'aimant qui fit mentir la boussole" (quoted in *Writer and Public in France*, p. 317). Balzac's *Illusions Perdues* (1843) describes the fortunes of an ambitious young writer during this earlier, less systematized stage of "industrial literature." It is against this background that

Zola measures subsequent developments in art and literature in *L'Œuvre* (1886).

4 The turning point in Britain was in 1894 with the ultimatum sent by Mudie's, the chief circulating library, to publishers who depended on its custom, requiring them to cease the production of triple-deckers. Gissing refers in his diary (Thursday, 9 August 1894) to "the recent Mudie revolution" (quoted in *London and the Life of Literature in Late Victorian England: The Diary of George Gissing*, p. 343).

5 This hardly-won measure, curbing the unrestricted "piracy" of books across national boundaries, was ratified by the Berne Convention of 1887 and the Platt-Simonds Bill which passed in the United States in 1891. Until this time, neither authors nor publishers had any control over foreign reprints.

6 *Writer and Public in France*, p. 296. Comparable figures apply to the London and New York presses.

7 See, for example: "The man of letters must make up his mind that in the United States the fate of a book is in the hands of the women. It is the women . . . who have the most leisure, and they read the most books" (*Literature and Life*, p. 21).

8 A number of short-lived organizations were formed in the United States; the most effective was the Authors' League, founded in 1891 with a president named Winston Churchill.

9 *Literature and Life*, p. 34.

10 *An Autobiography*, p. 323.

11 ibid., p. 271.

12 ibid., p. 356.

13 *Literature and Life*, pp. 32-3.

14 ibid., p. 3.

15 ibid., p. 1.

16 *Biographia Literaria*, p. 152.

17 *Literature and Life*, p. 1. Somewhat different considerations apply to women. While writing was one of the few professions (as opposed to factory and service jobs) in which they were represented, their relation to both aesthetic and commercial systems of value was marked by the general disparagement of the "woman writer" as qualitatively inferior, congenitally lacking in creative genius. Incapacity and inferiority were basic assumptions about women who wrote and categories to which they were usually

consigned automatically even if they achieved success. For men, making a decent living was prerequisite to masculine self-respect, but women who made large sums of money were considered to be symbolically stepping outside their proper domestic sphere, acting like a man.

18 *An Autobiography*, p. 271.
19 ibid., p. 278.
20 ibid., p. 329. Significantly, Trollope associates authors' beliefs in the special nature of their calling with a lack of masculinity. To treat art as something other than normal breadwinning work, something with its own unpredictable rhythms and flows, is to slacken off into weak effeminacy.
21 "Il a besoin de *ne rien faire*, pour faire quelque chose de son art. Il faut qu'il ne fasse rien d'utile et de journalier pour avoir le temps d'écouter les accords qui se forment lentement dans son âme, et que le bruit grossier d'un travail positif et régulier interrompt et fait infailliblement évanouir. – C'est LE POÈTE." (*Chatterton*, 1835, quoted in *Writer and Public in France*, p. 301).
22 *Literature and Life*, p. 4.
23 ibid., p. 5.
24 ibid., p. 5.
25 For details of authors' earning, see *Writer and Public in France*, pp. 301-32, and *Victorian Novelists and Publishers*, pp. 78-98.
26 *Literature and Life*, p. 34.
27 See Swanberg, *Dreiser*, pp. 156-7.
28 Dreiser, *Letters*, vol. I, p. 183 (30 November 1914).

Chapter 7

1 *New Grub Street*, ed. Bernard Bergonzi, Harmondsworth, Penguin, 1968, ch. VIII, p. 138. Page numbers, preceded by chapter references, will be given within the text from this edition, which reproduces the text of 1891.
2 In a less overtly exploitative mode, the naturalist project of classifying and writing about a range of social types, including women, resembles Jasper's scheme. Such a project could also be seen as a means to social control or social amelioration, and Zola's initial model of naturalism on the analogy of medical science begins with sweeping confidence in

the practical utility and high morality of our naturalist works, which experiment on man, dismantling the human machine piece by piece and putting it together again, to get it to work under the influence of its various environments. When time has moved on and we are in possession of the laws, it will simply be a matter of acting upon individuals and environments if we want to achieve the best possible social arrangements. (*Le Roman éxperimental*, p. 76)

(l'utilité pratique et la haute morale de nos œuvres naturalistes, qui expérimentent sur l'homme, qui démontent et remontent pièce à pièce la machine humaine, pour la faire fonctionner sous l'influence des milieux. Quand les temps auront marché, quand on possédera les lois, il n'y aura q'à agir sur les individus et sur les milieux, si l'on veut arriver au meilleur état social.)

The study of women with a view to curing their ills was carried out from both social and medical or psychiatric perspectives during this period of feminist agitation and the "New Woman." Reviewing *The Odd Women*, Gissing's own study of contemporary women, *The Woman's Herald* was enthusiastic about both its accuracy and its political usefulness: "No novel perhaps . . . has treated more exhaustively and more adequately the whole position of women . . . In displaying the evils of the present system, he undoubtedly points the way to a better state of things" (22 June 1893).

3   *Cf.* Jameson: "One of the structures by which Gissing can seek at least partially to relativize the finality of individual destinies is a use of echoing subplots in which the protagonists of each offer a *combinatoire* of the objective variants still possible in this increasingly closed universe" (*The Political Unconscious*, p. 96).

4   *Cf.* Raymond Williams, *The Long Revolution*, and Poole, *Gissing in Context*. The latter book contains two excellent chapters on the cultural background to *New Grub Street*, which are complemented by the more formalistic and expressly political analysis of Goode in *George Gissing: Ideology and Fiction*, pp. 109-41. A number of articles on the novel are collected in the second part of Michaux (ed.), *George Gissing: Critical Essays*, pp. 123–211. Tindall's *The Born Exile* and Halperin's *Gissing: A Life in Books* have largely psychobiographical readings of the novel.

5 *Cf.* Milvain on Jedwood: "Advertises hugely; he has the whole back page of *The Study* about every other week. I suppose Miss Wilkes's profits are paying for it" (XII, 193-4). There was a massive expansion of the advertising industry in the 1890s, utilizing both urban poster hoardings and the new popular press. See Turner, *The Shocking History of Advertising* and Nevett, *Advertising in Britain: A History*.

6 On popular culture in the 1890s, see Chanan, *The Dream that Kicks: The Prehistory and Early Years of Cinema in Britain*.

7 George Gissing, p. 116.

8 The title of this chapter is inspired by that of Norman Podhoretz's autobiography.

9 See ch. IX, p. 151.

10 *London and the Life of Literature in Late Victorian England*, p. 327.

11 ibid., pp. 232, 145, 150, 222, 430, 154.

12 See ch. IV, p. 81, where Reardon resumes the Coleridgean position:

> "How I envy those clerks who go by to their offices in the morning! There's the day's work cut out for them; no question of mood and feeling; they just have to work *at* something, and when the evening comes, they have earned their wages, they are free to rest and enjoy themselves. What an insane thing it is to make literature one's only means of support!"

See also Gissing in a letter of 1882:

> I often wish I were a carpenter, or a builder, or something of the kind; then at least one would sit down at night with the cheering consciousness of "something accomplished, something done," and the years would not seem a blank. (*Letters of George Gissing to Members of His Family*, p. 110)

13 *London and the Life of Literature in Late Victorian England*, p. 145.

14 ibid., p. 148.

15 See also Jameson: "Gissing forces a situation in which the universal commodification of desire stamps any achieved desire or wish as inauthentic, while an authenticity at best pathetic clings to images of failure" (*The Political Unconscious*, p. 204).

16 *London and the Life of Literature in Victorian England*, p. 471.
17 7 May 1882; *Letters*, pp. 113-14. *Cf.* J.-K. Huysmans, *À Rebours* (1884), where the narrator cancels a trip to England for fear of allowing reality to spoil the "Londres fictif" of his imagination (Paris, Garnier-Flammarion, 1978, p. 170).
18 It happened to Gissing, too.
19 The concept of sincerity became crucial in Gissing's later critical writings. See, for example, "The place of realism in fiction": "Sincerity I regard as of chief importance . . . Art, in the sense of craftsman's skill, without sincerity of vision will not suffice" (*George Gissing on Fiction*, p. 84).
20 ibid., pp. 70-1.

Chapter 8

1 "The New York Society for the Suppression of Vice." For details, see Swanberg, *Theodore Dreiser*, pp. 203-4.
2 The most extensive recent reading is in Pizer, *The Novels of Theodore Dreiser: A Critical Study*, pp. 133-52. Lehan gives much comparative biographical information in *Theodore Dreiser: His World and his Novels*.
3 Larzer Ziff, "Afterword" to Theodore Dreiser, *The "Genius"*, New York, Signet, 1967, p. 719.
4 Quoted in Salzman (ed.), *Theodore Dreiser: The Critical Reception*, p. 236.
5 ibid., pp. 227-8. British critics were often opposed to Dreiser's compatriots: witness the enthusiastic reception to Heinemann's 1901 edition of *Sister Carrie*.
6 ibid., p. 252.
7 *The "Genius"*, New York, Signet, 1967, book II, ch. V, p. 218. Page references from this edition, preceded by book and chapter numbers, will be given within the text.
8 It was not published until 1931.
9 ibid., pp. 8-9.
10 ibid., p. 9.
11 Here, the artistic inflection of a conventional distinction of gender adds force to the words of Christina Channing, the New York opera singer with whom Witla enjoys an idyllic vacation, who says that "they ought to get a new sex for artists" (I, XXIII, 148). It also

throws light on Dreiser's own perception of "that aggressiveness or superiority which so often characterizes the female artist" (*A Traveler*, p. 233).

12 *Critical Reception*, p. 240.
13 *A Traveler*, pp. 41-2.
14 ibid., p. 160.
15 See book I, chapters XVII-XIX.
16 *Critical Reception*, p. 241.

Chapter 9

1 *L'Œuvre*, ed. Antoinette Ehrard, Paris, Garnier-Flammarion, 1974, ch. XI, p. 367. All further references appear in the text.
2 "L'homme de génie nécessaire, celui qui incarnerait la formule en chefs d'œuvre. Quelle place à prendre! dompter la foule, ouvrir un siècle, créer un art!"
3 "Puis le pessimisme: pourtant, la foil l'acte générateur divinisé au fond. Et les contradictions, un commencement d'évolution, un début du 20ème siècle: de là, les efforts inutiles, les luttes de Claude" (*Ébauche*, Bibliothèque Nationale, NAF, ms. 10.316, fols. 276-7).
4 "J'en ferai naturellement un naturaliste, mais il faudrait le prendre avec sa personnalité" (ibid., fol. 274).
5 "La vérité est que les quelques jeunes romanciers que l'on croit écraser sous l'épithète commune de naturaliste, ont précisément les tempéraments les plus opposés qu'on puisse voir, pas un n'apporte la même personnalité, pas un ne regarde l'humanité sous le même angle" (*Le Roman éxpérimental*, p. 251).
6 The novel was published in 1886.
7 "C'est une époque qui s'achève, l'époque de Zola disciple. Mais c'est aussi le départ d'êtres humains; c'est la présence de la mort" (*"L'Œuvre" d'Émile Zola*). Brady's book and Niess's *Zola, Cézanne and Manet: A Study of "L'Œuvre"* are invaluable resources in reading *L'Œuvre*.
8 They were published in 1877 and 1880, respectively. By 1882, *Nana* had sold over 100,000 copies. "Certains succès romanesques représentent par leur tirage le volume de toute la production de la première moitié du siècle" (Charle, *La Crise littéraire à l'époque du naturalisme*, p. 43).

9 The authors were Alexis, Céard, Hennique, Huysmans, Maupassant and Zola.

10 "La fidélité au groupe est inversement proportionelle à la rapidité du succès" (*La Crise*, p. 66).

11 ibid., pp. 33-6, 61-4, *et passim*.

12 In *Le Roman éxpérimental*, pp. 177-210.

13 "Le livre, qui était un objet de luxe, devient un objet de consommation courante" ("L'Argent," p. 191).

14 "Des moyens nouveaux d'existence sont donnés à l'écrivain; et tout de suite l'idée d'hiérarchie s'en va, l'intelligence devient une noblesse, le travail se fait une dignité. En même temps, par une conséquence logique, l'influence des salons et de l'Académie disparaît" (ibid., p. 200).

15 "L'argent tue l'esprit" (ibid., p. 177). The conferring of literary prestige at this time was still in the hands of the old academies and state institutions, whose belletristic preferences were unchanged. Zola was on the lists to receive an official decoration in 1879, after the success of *L'Assommoir*, but his name was removed after he published an article construed as critical of the regime.

16 "Les livres et les pièces ne sont pas des objets de consommation courante, comme des chapeaux et des souliers par exemple . . . Non, en tout ceci, le génie seul importe. Il n'y a pas d'excuse aux encouragements . . . .

Il n'y a plus qu'à laisser aller les choses, car on ne donne du talent à personne, et le talent apporte justement avec lui la puissance nécessaire à son développement complet" (ibid., p. 208).

17 "La grande loi de la vie est la lutte, on ne vous doit rien, vous triompherez nécessairement si vous êtes une force . . . . Ensuite, ayez le respect de l'argent, ne tombez pas dans cet enfantillage de déblatérer en poètes contre lui" (ibid., p. 209).

18 "Génie incomplet" (*Ébauche*, fol. 10).

19 "Un absolu dédain pour tout ce qui n'était pas de la peinture."

20 "Est-ce que, en art, il y avait autre chose que de donner ce qu'on avait dans le ventre? . . . Est-ce qu'une botte de carottes, oui, une botte de carottes! étudiée directement, peinte naïvement, dans la note personelle où on la voit, ne valait pas les éternelles tartines de l'École, cette peinture au jus de chique, honteusement cuisinée d'après les recettes?"

21 "Ambition à désirer tout voir, tout faire, tout conquérir."

22 "Il m'a bien volé mon originalité! Croyez-vous que ça m'amuse, d'entendre, à chaque tableau, répéter derrière moi, depuis quinze ans: 'C'est un Claude!' "

23 – "Tous maintenant t'imitent, depuis ton *Plein Air*, dont ils ont tant ri... Regarde, regarde! ... De la main, au travers des salles, il désignait des toiles. En effet, le coup de clarté, peu à peu introduit dans la peinture contemporaine, éclatait enfin . . . Les vieux sujets académiques s'en étaient allés, avec les jus recuits de la tradition . . .

    – Ah! ta part est belle encore, mon vieux! continua Sandoz. L'art de demain sera le tien, tu les a tous faits."

24 "Il bénéficiait de toute la haine qu'on avait contre eux, on couvrait d'éloges ses toiles adoucies, pour achever de tuer leurs oeuvres obstinément violentes."

25 The earlier picture is described exactly like Manet's *Déjeuner sur l'herbe*, and the scene, as the *Ébauche* makes clear, is based on the Salon des Refusés of 1863.

26 "C'était le tableau de Fagerolles. Et il retrouvait son *Plein air*, dans ce *Déjeuner*, la même note blonde, la même formule d'art, mais combien adoucie, truquée, gâtée, d'une élégance d'épiderme, arrangée avec une adresse infinie pour les satisfactions basses du public."

27 "Ruse de sauvage, pour emporter à bas prix la toile qu'il convoitait."

28 "Un spéculateur, un boursier . . . il devinait l'artiste à lancer, non pas celui qui promettait le génie discuté d'un grand peintre, mais celui dont le talent menteur . . . allait faire prime sur le marché bourgeois. Et c'était ainsi qu'il bouleversait le marché, en écartant l'ancien amateur de goût et en ne traitant plus qu'avec l'amateur riche, qui ne se connaît pas en art, qui achète un tableau comme une valeur de Bourse, par vanité ou dans l'espoir qu'elle montera."

29 Naudet practices an interesting fiddle which he calls "le coup de l'Américain." It involves falsely claiming, and thereby eventually producing, record prices for a given artist's work and recalls, from the other point of view, the indiscriminate, inflated purchases made by James's Newman in *The American* (1876).

30 "Une jolie génération de peintres calqueurs, doublés d'hommes d'affaires malhonnêtes."

31 "Et quelle publicité! un charivari d'un bout de la France à l'autre, de soudaines renommées qui poussent du soir au matin, et qui éclatent en coups de foudre, au milieu des populations béantes. Sans parler des œuvres, ces pauvres œuvres annoncées par des salves d'artillerie attendues dans un délire d'impatience, enrageant Paris pendant huit jours, puis tombant à l'éternel oubli."

32 "L'écrivain, en effet, venait de publier un nouveau roman; et, bien que la critique ne désarmait pas, il se faisait enfin, autour de ce dernier, cette rumeur du succès qui consacre un homme, sous les attaques persistantes de ses adversaires. D'ailleurs, il n'avait aucune illusion, il savait bien que la bataille, même gagnée, recommencerait à chacun de ses livres. Le grand travail de sa vie avançait, cette série de romans, ces volumes qu'il lançait coup sur coup, d'une main obstinée et régulière, marchant au but qu'il s'était donné, sans se laisser vaincre par rien, obstacles, injures, fatigues."

33 "Ecoute, le travail a pris mon existence . . . Plus rien, plus rien dans mon trou que le travail et moi . . .!"

34 "La vente de ses livres augmentait, le faisait riche; l'appartement de la rue de Londres prenait un grand luxe, à côté de la petite maison bourgeoise des Batignolles; et lui restait immuable."

35 "L'accession du roman au rang de genre dominant est une transformation fondamentale du champ littéraire. Techniquement, les gros tirages de production deviennent possible sous le Second Empire; socialement, le roman trouve un nouveau public intermédiaire entre le public parisien et lettré et le public populaire du roman. Ce public ne va pas au théâtre, mais il accède néanmoins à la culture légitime grâce à cette forme de consommation culturelle privée et domestique" (*La Crise*, p. 37). "The accession of the novel to the position of dominant genre is a fundamental transformation of the literary field. Technically, large print-runs become possible under the Second Empire; socially, the novel finds a new, intermediate public between the lettered Paris public and the novel's lower-class public. This public does not visit the theatre, but it gains access nonetheless to established culture, thanks to this private, domestic form of cultural consumption."

36 "Notre génération est trop encrassée de lyrisme pour laisser des

Notes

œuvres saines . . . Seule, la vérite, la nature, est la base possible, la police nécessaire, en dehors de laquelle la folie commence; et qu'on ne craigne pas d'aplatir l'œuvre, le tempérament est là, qui emportera toujours le créateur."

37 "Ah, j'ai trouvé ce qu'il me fallait, à moi. Oh! pas grand-chose, un petit coin seulement, ce qui suffit pour une vie humaine."

Postscript

1 See Madeleine B. Stern, *Purple Passage: The Life of Mrs Frank Leslie*, Norman, University of Oklahoma Press, 1953.
2 *Experiment in Autobiography*, New York, Macmillan, 1934, p. 417.
3 *Dream Worlds.*
4 In Fox and Lears (eds), *The Culture of Consumption: Critical Essays in American History 1880-1980*, pp. 65-100.
5 Preface to *The Picture of Dorian Gray* (1890), p. xxxiv.

Short bibliography
of secondary works

Abrams, Philip, *The Origins of British Sociology*, Chicago, University of Chicago Press, 1968.

Adburgham, Alison, *Liberty's: A Biography of a Shop*, London, Allen and Unwin, 1975.

—— *Shopping in Style: London from the Restoration to Edwardian Elegance*, London, Thames and Hudson, 1975.

Althusser, Louis, *Lenin and Philosophy and Other Essays*, trans. Ben Brewster, London, New Left Books, 1971.

Altick, Richard D., *The English Common Reader: A Social History of the Mass Reading Public 1800-1900*, Chicago, University of Chicago Press, 1957.

Auerbach, Nina, *Communities of Women: An Idea in Fiction*, Cambridge, Harvard University Press, 1978.

Avenel, Georges d', "Le mécanisme de la vie moderne," *Revue des Deux Mondes*, vol. CXXIV, July 1894, 329-69.

Barrett, Michèle, *Women's Oppression Today: Problems in Marxist Feminist Analysis*, London, Verso, 1980.

Barth, Gunther, *City People*, New York, Oxford University Press, 1982.

Barthes, Roland, *Mythologies*, Paris, Le Seuil, 1957.

—— *Système de la mode*, Paris, Le Seuil, 1967.

Baudrillard, Jean, *La Société de consommation*, 1970, repr. Paris, Gallimard, coll. "Idees," 1976.

Bibliography

—— *Le Système des objets*, 1968, repr. Paris, Denoël Gonthier, coll. *Méditations*, 1981.

Becker, George G., *Documents of Modern Literary Realism*, Princeton, Princeton University Press, 1963.

Benjamin, Walter, *Illuminations*, ed. Hannah Arendt, trans. Harry Zohn, New York, Schocken Books, 1969.

—— *Reflections*, ed. Peter Demetz, trans. Edmund Jephcott, New York, Harcourt Brace Jovanovich, 1978.

—— *One-Way Street and Other Writings*, trans. Edmund Jephcott and Kingsley Shorter, London, New Left Books, 1979.

—— "A short history of photography," trans. Stanley Mitchell, *Screen*, 13, no. 1, Spring 1972, 5-26.

Benson, Susan Porter, "Powers of consumption and machine for selling: the American department store 1880-1940," *Radical History Review*, 21, Fall 1979, 199-221.

Berger, John, *Ways of Seeing*, Harmondsworth, Pelican, 1972.

Bok, E.W., "Literary factories," *Publishers' Weekly*, no. 1072, 13 August 1892.

Boorstin, Daniel, *The Americans: The Democratic Experience*, New York, Random House, 1973.

—— *The Image: A Guide to Pseudo-Events in America*, 1961, repr. New York, Atheneum, 1971.

Bourdieu, Pierre, *Questions de sociologie*, Paris, Minuit, 1981.

Bouvier-Ajam, Maurice, "Zola et les magasins de nouveauté," *Europe*, avril-mai 1968, 47-54.

Brady, Patrick, *"L'Œuvre" d'Émile Zola*, Geneva, Librairie Droz, 1968.

Chanan, Michael, *The Dream that Kicks: The Prehistory and Early Years of Cinema in Britain*, London, Routledge & Kegan Paul, 1980.

Charle, Christophe, *La Crise littéraire à l'époque du naturalisme*, Paris, Presses de l'École Normale Supérieure, 1979.

Chevrel, Yves, *Le Naturalisme*, Paris, Presses Universitaires de France, 1982.

Chirot, Daniel, *Social Change in the Twentieth Century*, New York, Harcourt Brace Jovanovich, 1977.

Cogny, Pierre, *Le Naturalisme*, Paris, Presses Universitaires de France, 1976.

Coleridge, S.T., *Biographia Literaria* (1817), ed. J. Shawcross, Oxford, Oxford University Press, 1907, 2 vols.

Colloque de Cerisy, *Le Naturalisme*, Paris, Union Générale d'Éditions, coll. 10/18, 1978.

Coser, Lewis A., Kadushin, Charles and Powell, Walter W., *Books: The Culture and Commerce of Publishing*, New York, Basic Books, 1982.

Coustillas, Pierre and Partridge, Colin, *Gissing: The Critical Heritage*, London Routledge & Kegan Paul, 1972.

Coward, Rosalind, *Patriarchal precedents: Sexuality and Social Relations*, London, Routledge & Kegan Paul, 1972.

Dale, Tim, *Harrods: The Store and the Legend*, London, Pan Books, 1981.

Dangerfield, George, *The Strange Death of Liberal England*, New York, Harrison Smith and Robert Haas, 1935.

Davis, Dorothy, *A History of Shopping*, London, Routledge & Kegan Paul, 1966.

Debord, Guy, *La Société du spectacle*, 1967, repr. Paris, Éditions champ libre, 1973.

Debray, Regis, *Le Pouvoir intellectuel en France*, Paris, Éditions Ramsay, 1979.

Delbourg-Delphis, Marylène, *Le Chic et le look*, Paris, Hachette, 1981.

Dézelay, Auguste (ed.), *Lectures de Zola*, Paris, Armand Colin, 1973.

Douglas, Ann, *The Feminization of American Culture*, New York, Avon, 1976.

Dreiser, Theodore, *American Diaries 1902-1926*, ed. Thomas P. Riggio, Philadelphia, University of Pennsylvania Press, 1982.

—— *Dawn*, New York, Horace Liveright, 1931.

—— *Letters*, ed. Robert H. Elias, Philadelphia, University of Pennsylvania Press, 1959.

—— *A Selection of Uncollected Prose*, ed. Donald Pizer, Detroit, Wayne State University Press, 1977.

—— *A Traveler at Forty*, New York, Harper & Row, 1913.

Dyer, Richard, *Stars*, London, British Film Institute, 1979.

Eagleton, Terry, *Criticism and Ideology*, London, New Left Books, 1976.

—— *Walter Benjamin or Towards a Revolutionary Criticism*, London, Verso, 1981.

—— *Literary Theory: An Introduction*, Minneapolis, University of Minnesota Press, 1983.

Bibliography

Elias, Robert H. (ed.), *Letters of Theodore Dreiser: A Selection*, 3 vols, Philadelphia, University of Pennsylvania Press, 1959.

—— *Theodore Dreiser: Apostle of Nature*, 2nd edn, Ithaca, Cornell University Press, 1970.

Ellis, John, *Visible Fictions: Cinema, Television, Video*, London, Routledge & Kegan Paul, 1982.

Erenberg, Lewis A., *Steppin' Out: New York Nightlife and the Transformation of American Culture 1890-1930*, Westport, Conn., Greenwood Press, 1982.

Ewen, Elizabeth and Ewen, Stuart, *Channels of Desire: Mass Images and the Shaping of American Consciousness*, New York, McGraw-Hill, 1982.

Ewen, Stuart, *Captains of Consciousness: Advertising and the Social Roots of the Consumer Culture*, 1975, repr. New York, McGraw-Hill, 1976.

Felman, Shoshana, *La Folie et la chose littéraire*, Paris, Le Seuil, 1978.

Foucault, Michel, *La Volonté de savoir*, Paris, Gallimard, 1977.

Fox, Richard Wightman and Lears, Jackson T. (eds), *The Culture of Consumption: Critical Essays in American History 1880-1980*, New York, Pantheon, 1983.

Franklin, Alfred, *Les Magasins de nouveauté*, Paris, Plon, 1896.

Fraser, W. Hamish, *The Coming of the Mass Market, 1850-1914*, London, Macmillan, 1981.

Freud, Sigmund, trans. James Strachey, *Complete Psychological Works, Standard Edition*, 24 vols, London, Hogarth Press, 1953-74.

Furst, Lilian R. and Skrine, Peter N., *Naturalism*, London, Methuen, 1971.

Gissing, A. and E. (eds), *Letters of George Gissing to Members of his Family*, London, Constable, 1927.

Gissing, George, *London and the Life of Literature in Late Victorian England: The Diary of George Gissing*, ed. Pierre Coustillas, Brighton, Harvester Press, 1978.

Goode, John, *George Gissing: Ideology and Fiction*, London, Vision Press, 1978.

Gurevitch, Michael, Bennet, T., Curran, J. and Woollacott, J. (eds), *Culture, Society and the Media*, London, Methuen, 1982.

Hall, Stuart, Hobson, Dorothy, Lowe, Andrew and Willis, Paul (eds), *Culture, Media, Language*, London, Hutchinson, 1980.

Just Looking

Halperin, John, *Gissing: A Life in Books*, Oxford, Oxford University Press, 1982.

Hemmings, F.W.J., *Culture and Society in France 1848-1898*, London, Batsford, 1971.

—— *The Life and Time of Emile Zola*, London, Elek, 1977.

—— *Emile Zola*, 2nd edn, Oxford, Clarendon Press, 1966.

Hendrickson, Robert, *The Grand Emporiums*, New York, Stein and Day, 1970.

Hoggart, Richard, *The Uses of Literacy*, London, Chatto and Windus, 1957.

Howells, William Dean, *Literature and Life*, New York, Harper, 1902.

Hungerford, Edward, *The Romance of a Great Store*, New York, Robert M. McBride, 1922.

Jameson, Fredric, *Marxism and Form*, Princeton, Princeton University Press, 1971.

—— *The Political Unconscious: Narrative as a Socially Symbolic Act*, London, Methuen, 1981.

Jennings, Chantal Bertrand, *L'Éros et la femme chez Zola*, Paris, Klincksieck, 1977.

Jones, Peter d'A., *The Consumer Society: A History of American Capitalism*, Harmondsworth, Penguin, 1965.

Kazin, Alfred and Shapiro, Charles (eds), *The Stature of Theodore Dreiser*, Bloomington, Indiana University Press, 1955.

Keating, P.J., *George Gissing, "New Grub Street"*, London, Edward Arnold, 1968.

—— *The Working Classes in Victorian Fiction*, London, Routledge & Kegan Paul, 1971.

Korg, Jacob, *George Gissing: A Critical Biography*, 1963, repr. Brighton, Harvester Press, 1980.

Korg, Jacob and Korg, Cynthia (eds), *George Gissing on Fiction*, London, Enitharmon Press, 1978.

Kuhn, Annette, *Women's Pictures: Feminism and Cinema*, London, Routledge & Kegan Paul, 1982.

Lacan, Jacques, *Écrits*, trans. Alan Sheridan, London, Tavistock, 1976.

Leavis, Q.D., *Fiction and the Reading Public*, 1932, repr. London, Chatto and Windus, 1968.

Leenhardt, Jacques and Josza, Pierre, *Lire la lecture*, Paris, Le Sycomore, 1982.

Bibliography

Lefebvre, Henri, *La Vie quotidienne dans le monde moderne*, 1968, repr. Paris, Gallimard, 1975.

Lehan, Richard, *Theodore Dreiser: His World and His Novels*, Carbondale, Southern Illinois University Press, 1969.

Lesselier, Claudie, "Employées de grands magasins à Paris (avant 1914)," *Le Mouvement social*, no. 105, 1978, 109–26.

Lough, John, *Writer and Public in France*, Oxford, Clarendon Press, 1978.

Lukács, Georg, *Studies in European Realism*, New York, Grosset and Dunlap, 1964.

—— *Writer and Critic*, ed. and trans. Arthur D. Kahn, London, Merlin Press, 1970.

Macherey, Pierre, *Towards a Theory of Literary Production*, trans. G. Wall, London, Routledge & Kegan Paul, 1978.

McKendrick, Neil, Brewer, John and Plumb, J.H., *The Birth of a Consumer Society: the Commercialization of Eighteenth-Century England*, Cambridge, Cambridge University Press, 1982.

Marrey, Bernard, *Les grands magasins*, Paris, Picard, 1979.

Martino, P., *Le Naturalisme francais*, Paris, Colin, 1923.

Marx, Karl, *Capital*, vol. I (1870), trans. Ben Fowkes, Harmondsworth, Penguin, 1976.

Michaux, Jean-Pierre (ed.), *George Gissing: Critical Essays*, London, Vision Press, 1981.

Michaels, Walter Benn, "*Sister Carrie*'s popular economy," *Critical Inquiry* 7, no. 2, Winter 1980, 373–90.

Miller, J. Hillis, *Fiction and Repetition: Seven English Novels*, Cambridge, Harvard University Press, 1982.

Miller, Michael B., *The Bon Marché: Bourgeois Culture and the Department Store, 1869–1920*, Princeton, Princeton University Press, 1981.

Mitchell, Juliet, *Psychoanalysis and Feminism*, 1973, repr. Harmondsworth, Penguin, 1974.

Moers, Ellen, *Two Dreisers*, New York, Viking Press, 1969.

Morin, Edgar, *Les Stars*, Paris, Le Seuil, 1972.

Mulhern, Francis, *The Moment of "Scrutiny"*, 1979, repr. New York, Schocken Books, 1982.

Nevett, T.R., *Advertising in Britain: A History*, London, Heinemann, 1982.

Niess, Robert J., *Zola, Cézanne and Manet: A Study of "L'Œuvre"*, Ann Arbor, University of Michigan Press, 1968.

Parent-Lardeur, Françoise, *Les Cabinets de lecture*, Paris, Payot, 1983.
―― *Les Demoiselles de magasin*, Paris, Éditions Ouvrières, 1969.
Pasdermadjian, H., *Le grand magasin*, Paris, Dunod, 1949.
Perrot, Philippe, *Les Dessus et les dessous de la bourgeoisie: Une histoire du vêtement au 19ème siècle*, Paris, Fayard, 1981.
Petrey, Sandy, "The language of realism, the language of false consciousness," *Novel*, 10, 1977, 101-13.
Pizer, Donald, *The Novels of Theodore Dreiser: A Critical Study*, Minneapolis, University of Minnesota Press, 1976.
―― *Realism and Naturalism in Nineteenth Century American Literature*, Carbondale, Southern Illinois University Press, 1966.
Poole, Adrian, *Gissing in Context*, London, Macmillan, 1975.
Psychanalyse et Cinema, ed. R. Bellour, T. Kuntzel, C. Matz, *Communications* 23 (1975).
Ripoll, Roger, *Réalité et mythe chez Zola*, Lille, Atelier réproduction des thèses, 1981.
Rockwell, Joan, *Fact in Fiction*, London, Routledge & Kegan Paul, 1974.
Salzman, Jack (ed.), *Theodore Dreiser: The Critical Reception*, New York, David Lewis, 1972.
Schor, Naomi, *Zola's Crowds*, Baltimore, Johns Hopkins University Press, 1978.
Sennett, Richard, *The Fall of Public Man*, New York, Vintage Books, 1974.
Serres, Michel, *Feux et signaux de brume: Zola*, Paris, Grasset, 1975.
Showalter, Elaine, *A Literature of Their Own: British Women Novelists from Bronte to Lessing*, Princeton, Princeton University Press, 1977.
Sundquist, Eric J. (ed.), *American Realism: New Essays*, Baltimore, Johns Hopkins University Press, 1982.
Sutherland, J.A., *Victorian Novelists and Publishers*, London, The Athlone Press, 1976.
Swanberg, W.A., *Dreiser*, New York, Scribner, 1965.
Tebbel, John, *A History of Book Publishing in the United States*, vol. II: *The Expansion of an Industry, 1865-1919*, New York, R.R. Bowker, 1975.
Thil, Étienne, *Les Inventeurs du commerce moderne*, Paris, Arthaud, 1966.

Bibliography

Tindall, Gillian, *The Born Exile: George Gissing*, London, Temple Smith, 1974.

Trachtenberg, Alan, *The Incorporation of America: Culture and Society in the Gilded Age*, New York, Hill & Wang, 1982.

Trent, William Peterfield, Erskine, John, Sherman, Stuart P. and Van Doren, Carl (eds), *The Cambridge History of American Literature*, 3 vols, New York, Macmillan, 1921.

Trollope, Anthony, *An Autobiography* (1883), ed. Michael Sadleir and Frederick Page, Oxford, Oxford University Press, 1980.

Turner, E.S., *The Shocking History of Advertising*, Harmondsworth, Penguin, 1965.

Veblen, Thorstein, *The Theory of the Leisure Class* (1899), repr. New York, Mentor, 1953.

Wendt, Lloyd and Kogan, Herman, *Give the Lady What She Wants*, Chicago, Rand McNally, 1952.

Wilde, Oscar, *The Picture of Dorian Gray* (1890), repr. London, Oxford University Press, 1974.

Williams, Raymond, *The Country and the City*, London, Fontana, 1973.

—— *Keywords: A Vocabulary of Culture and Society*, London, Fontana, 1976.

—— *The Long Revolution*, London, Chatto and Windus, 1961.

Williams, Rosalind H., *Dream Worlds: Mass Consumption in Late Nineteenth-Century France*, Berkeley, University of California Press, 1982.

Woolf, Virginia, *Three Guineas* (1938), repr. New York, Harcourt, 1966.

—— *A Room of One's Own* (1929), repr. London, Hogarth Press, 1959; Toronto, Clarke, Irwin & Co.

Zeldin, Theodore, *France, 1848-1945*, 5 vols, Oxford, Oxford University Press, 1979-81.

Zola, ed. Naomi Shaw, *Yale French Studies* 42 (1969).

Zola, Émile, *Mon Salon, Manet*, Paris, Garnier-Flammarion, 1970.

—— *Le Roman expérimental* (1880) Paris, Garnier-Flammarion, 1971.

Index

References to the notes on pages 155–75 are indicated by reference to both
the page and note number in parentheses, e.g. Fox, R.W., 175n.(4)
*Passim is used to indicate scattered references to the subject throughout the indicated
pages of text, e.g. art versus commerce, 98–117 passim*

184